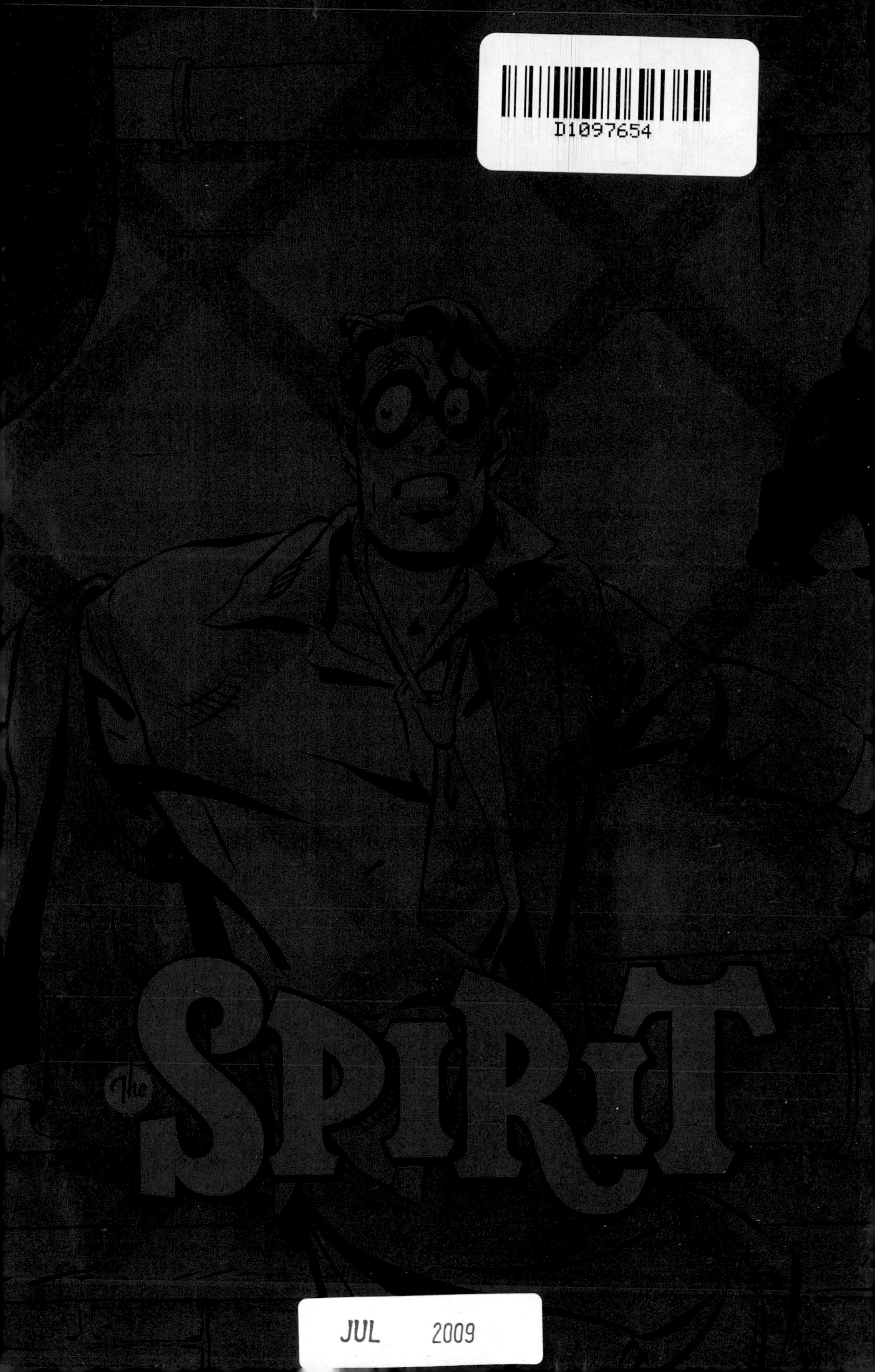

The SPIRIT

THE SPIRIT Book Three Published by DC Comics. Cover and compilation Copyright © 2009 Will Eisner Studios, Inc. All Rights Reserved.
THE SPIRIT, images of Denny Colt, Commissioner Dolan and Ebony are registered trademarks of Will Eisner Studios, Inc.

Originally published in single magazine form in THE SPIRIT 14-20 Copyright © 2008 and Will Eisner Studios, Inc. The stories, characters and
incidents featured in this publication are entirely fictional. DC Comics does not read or accept unsolicited submissions of ideas, stories or artwork.

SFI
CERTIFIED
SOURCING
PWC-SFICOC-260
Fiber used in this product line meets the
sourcing requirements of the SFI program.
www.sfiprogram.org

DC Comics, 1700 Broadway, New York, NY 10019
A Warner Bros. Entertainment Company
Printed in Canada. First Printing.
ISBN:978-1-4012-2186-7

Writers
Sergio Aragonés
Mark Evanier

Artists
Mike Ploog & Mark Farmer
Paul Smith
Aluir Amancio & Terry Austin
Paul Smith & Walden Wong
Jason Armstrong
Paul Rivoche

Colors by
Dave Stewart
Lee Loughridge
Paul Rivoche

Letters by
Rob Leigh & Todd Klein

The Spirit created by Will Eisner

The SPIRIT

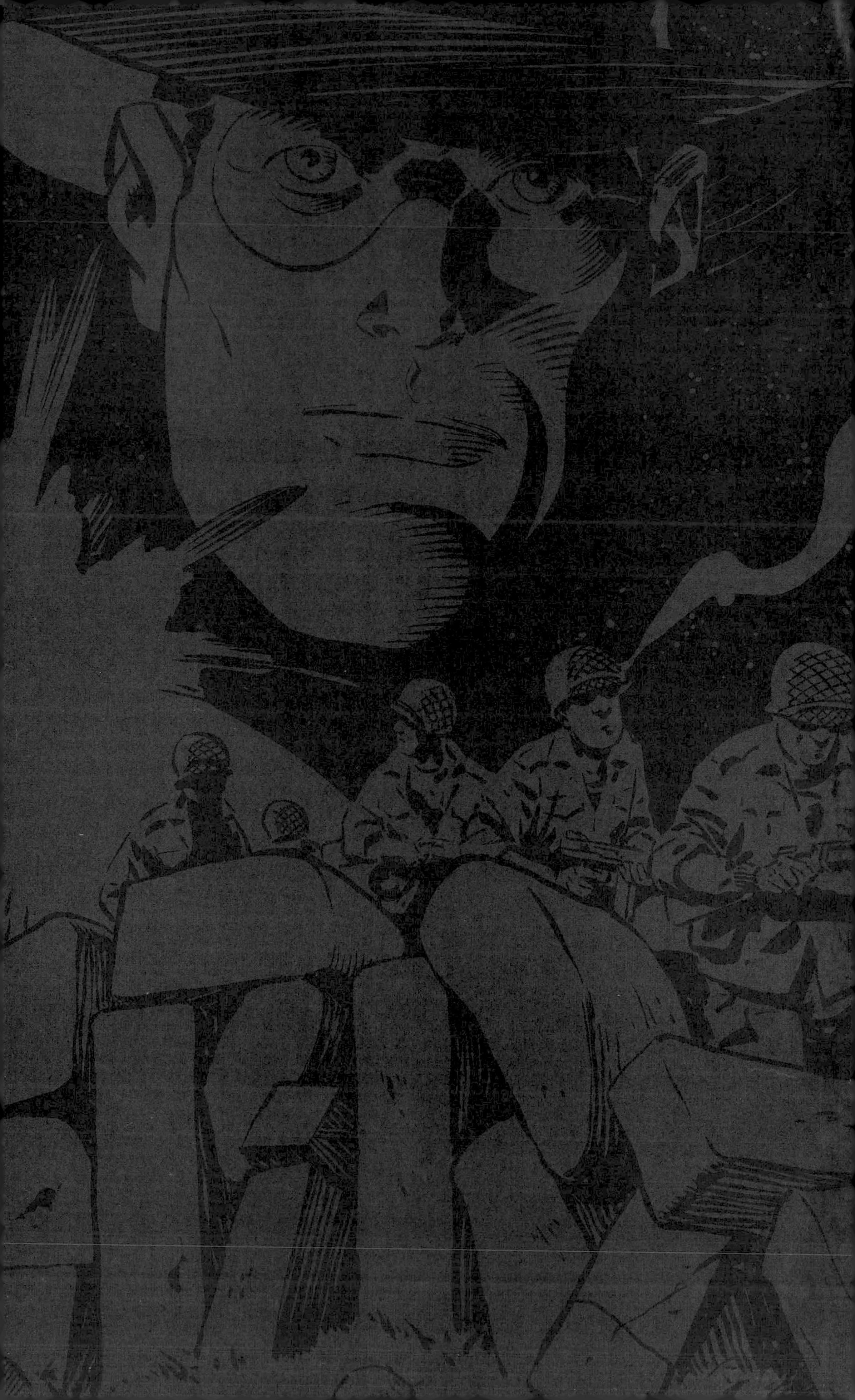

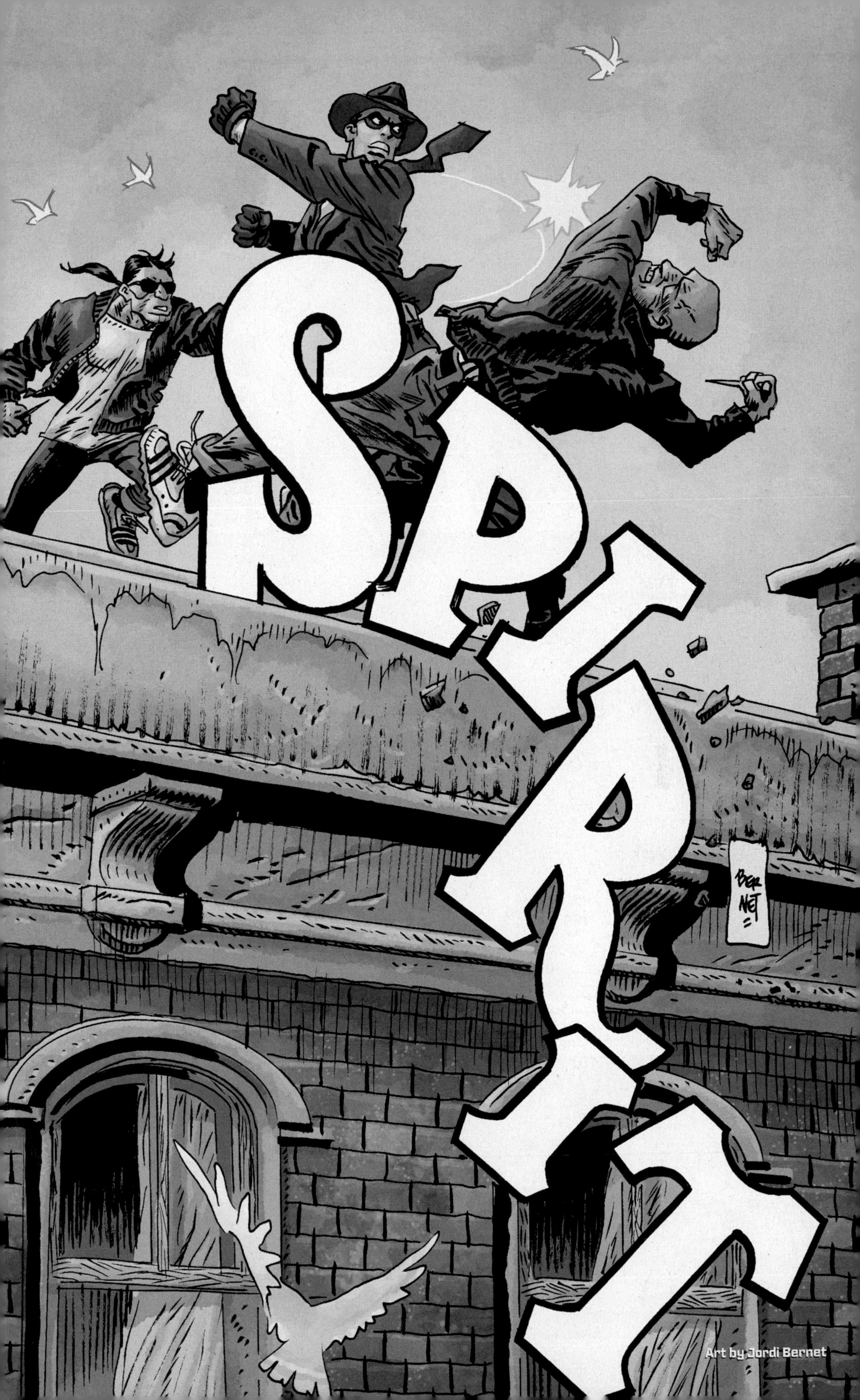
SPIRIT
Art by Jordi Bernet

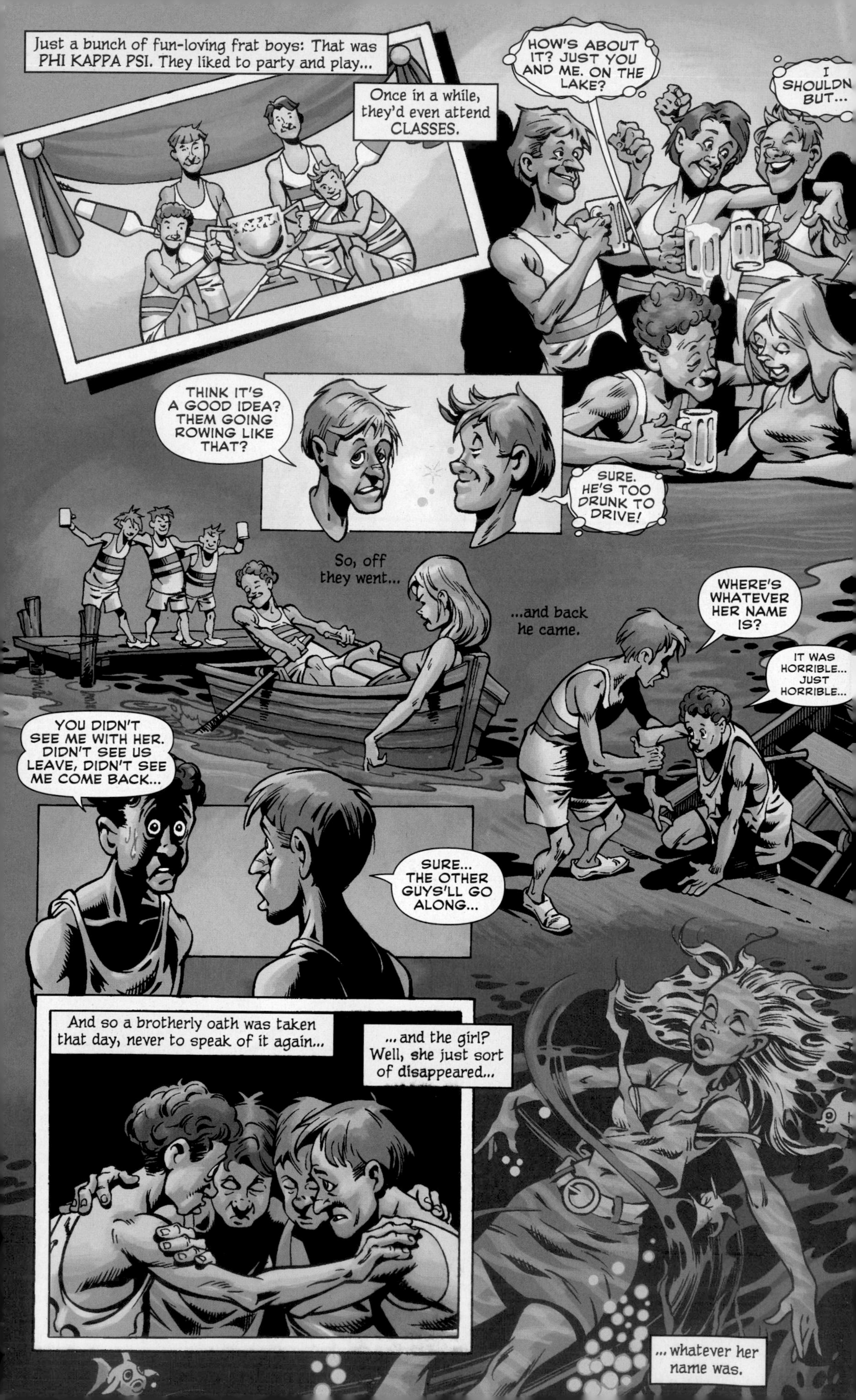

Just a bunch of fun-loving frat boys: That was PHI KAPPA PSI. They liked to party and play...
Once in a while, they'd even attend CLASSES.
HOW'S ABOUT IT? JUST YOU AND ME. ON THE LAKE?
I SHOULDN BUT...
THINK IT'S A GOOD IDEA? THEM GOING ROWING LIKE THAT?
SURE. HE'S TOO DRUNK TO DRIVE!
So, off they went...
...and back he came.
WHERE'S WHATEVER HER NAME IS?
IT WAS HORRIBLE... JUST HORRIBLE...
YOU DIDN'T SEE ME WITH HER. DIDN'T SEE US LEAVE, DIDN'T SEE ME COME BACK...
SURE... THE OTHER GUYS'LL GO ALONG...
And so a brotherly oath was taken that day, never to speak of it again...
...and the girl? Well, she just sort of disappeared...
...whatever her name was.

THE MEDICAL MURDERS

THE SPIRIT

But that was then. This is now...

YOU HEAR, BOSS? ANOTHER DOCTOR MURDERED!

I HEARD, I HEARD...

TO THE SCENE OF THE CRIME?

WHERE ELSE?

WE COULD STOP OFF AT VITO'S PIZZERIA... MAYBE SPLIT ONE OF HIS "DEATH BY MOZZARELLA" SPECIALS...

NOT TONIGHT, EB...

IF I PUT ON ANY MORE WEIGHT, I'LL HAVE TO HAVE MY MASK LET OUT. BESIDES, I HAVE A TEXT MESSAGE FROM DOLAN...

...SOUNDS LIKE HE NEEDS ME SOMETHING BAD.

JUST KEEP VITO'S IN MIND, OKAY?

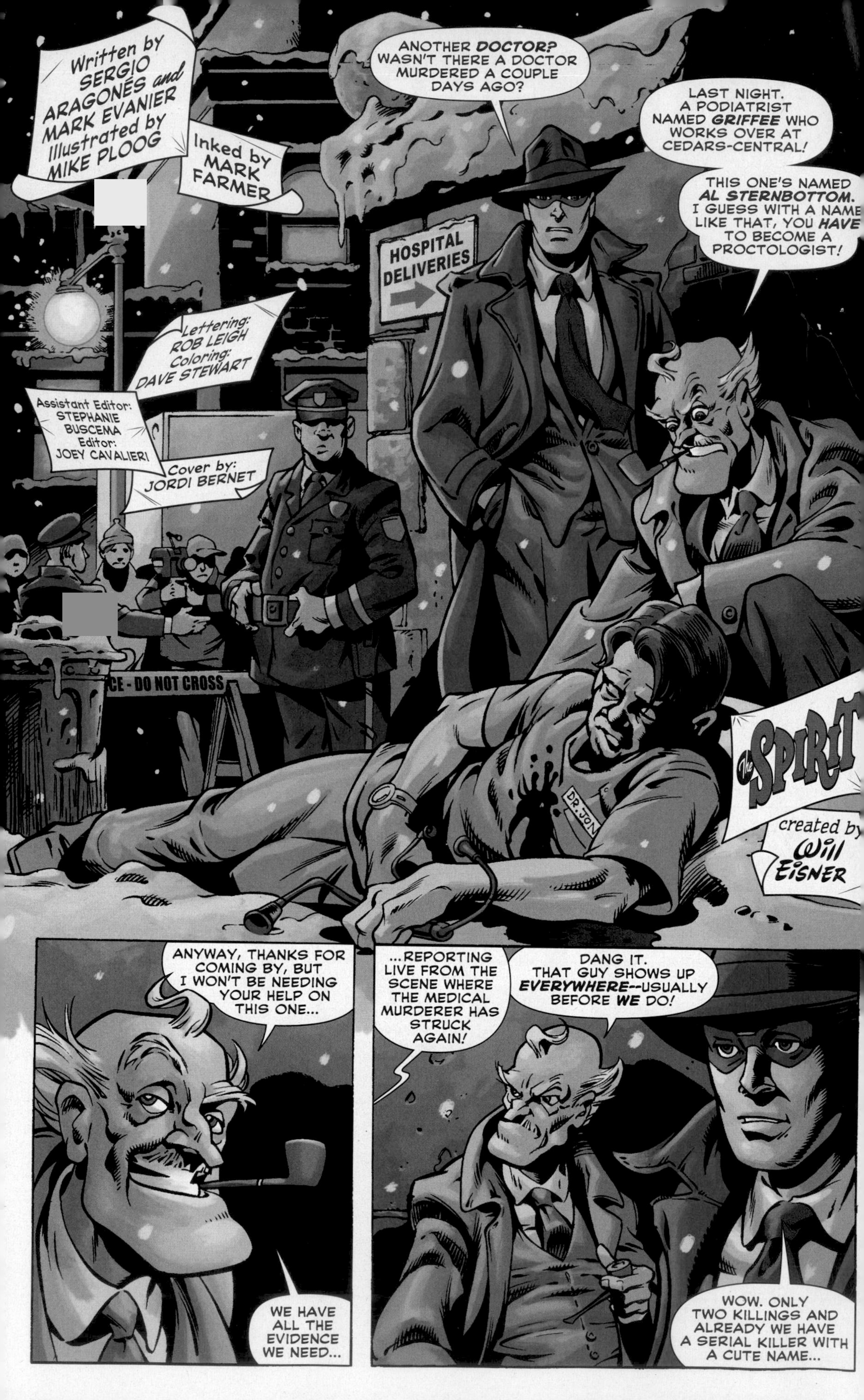

Written by SERGIO ARAGONÉS and MARK EVANIER
Illustrated by MIKE PLOOG
Inked by MARK FARMER
Lettering: ROB LEIGH
Coloring: DAVE STEWART
Assistant Editor: STEPHANIE BUSCEMA
Editor: JOEY CAVALIERI
Cover by: JORDI BERNET
HOSPITAL DELIVERIES
ANOTHER DOCTOR? WASN'T THERE A DOCTOR MURDERED A COUPLE DAYS AGO?
LAST NIGHT. A PODIATRIST NAMED GRIFFEE WHO WORKS OVER AT CEDARS-CENTRAL!
THIS ONE'S NAMED AL STERNBOTTOM. I GUESS WITH A NAME LIKE THAT, YOU HAVE TO BECOME A PROCTOLOGIST!
CE - DO NOT CROSS
DR. JON
The SPIRIT
created by Will Eisner
ANYWAY, THANKS FOR COMING BY, BUT I WON'T BE NEEDING YOUR HELP ON THIS ONE...
WE HAVE ALL THE EVIDENCE WE NEED...
...REPORTING LIVE FROM THE SCENE WHERE THE MEDICAL MURDERER HAS STRUCK AGAIN!
DANG IT. THAT GUY SHOWS UP EVERYWHERE--USUALLY BEFORE WE DO!
WOW. ONLY TWO KILLINGS AND ALREADY WE HAVE A SERIAL KILLER WITH A CUTE NAME...

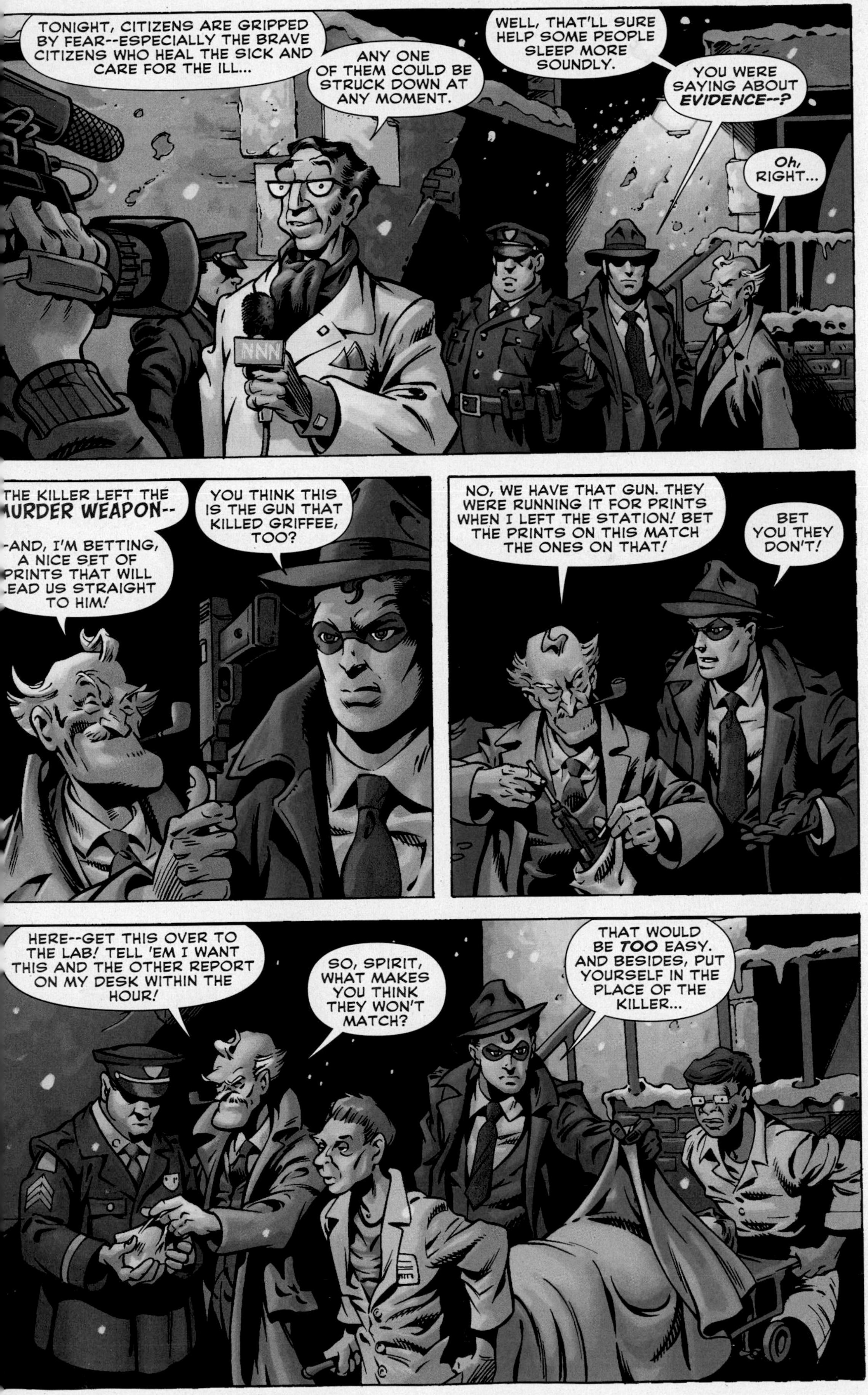
TONIGHT, CITIZENS ARE GRIPPED BY FEAR--ESPECIALLY THE BRAVE CITIZENS WHO HEAL THE SICK AND CARE FOR THE ILL...
ANY ONE OF THEM COULD BE STRUCK DOWN AT ANY MOMENT.
NNN
WELL, THAT'LL SURE HELP SOME PEOPLE SLEEP MORE SOUNDLY.
YOU WERE SAYING ABOUT *EVIDENCE--?*
Oh, RIGHT...
THE KILLER LEFT THE URDER WEAPON--
-AND, I'M BETTING, A NICE SET OF PRINTS THAT WILL EAD US STRAIGHT TO HIM!
YOU THINK THIS IS THE GUN THAT KILLED GRIFFEE, TOO?
NO, WE HAVE THAT GUN. THEY WERE RUNNING IT FOR PRINTS WHEN I LEFT THE STATION! BET THE PRINTS ON THIS MATCH THE ONES ON THAT!
BET YOU THEY DON'T!
HERE--GET THIS OVER TO THE LAB! TELL 'EM I WANT THIS AND THE OTHER REPORT ON MY DESK WITHIN THE HOUR!
SO, SPIRIT, WHAT MAKES YOU THINK THEY WON'T MATCH?
THAT WOULD BE *TOO* EASY. AND BESIDES, PUT YOURSELF IN THE PLACE OF THE KILLER...

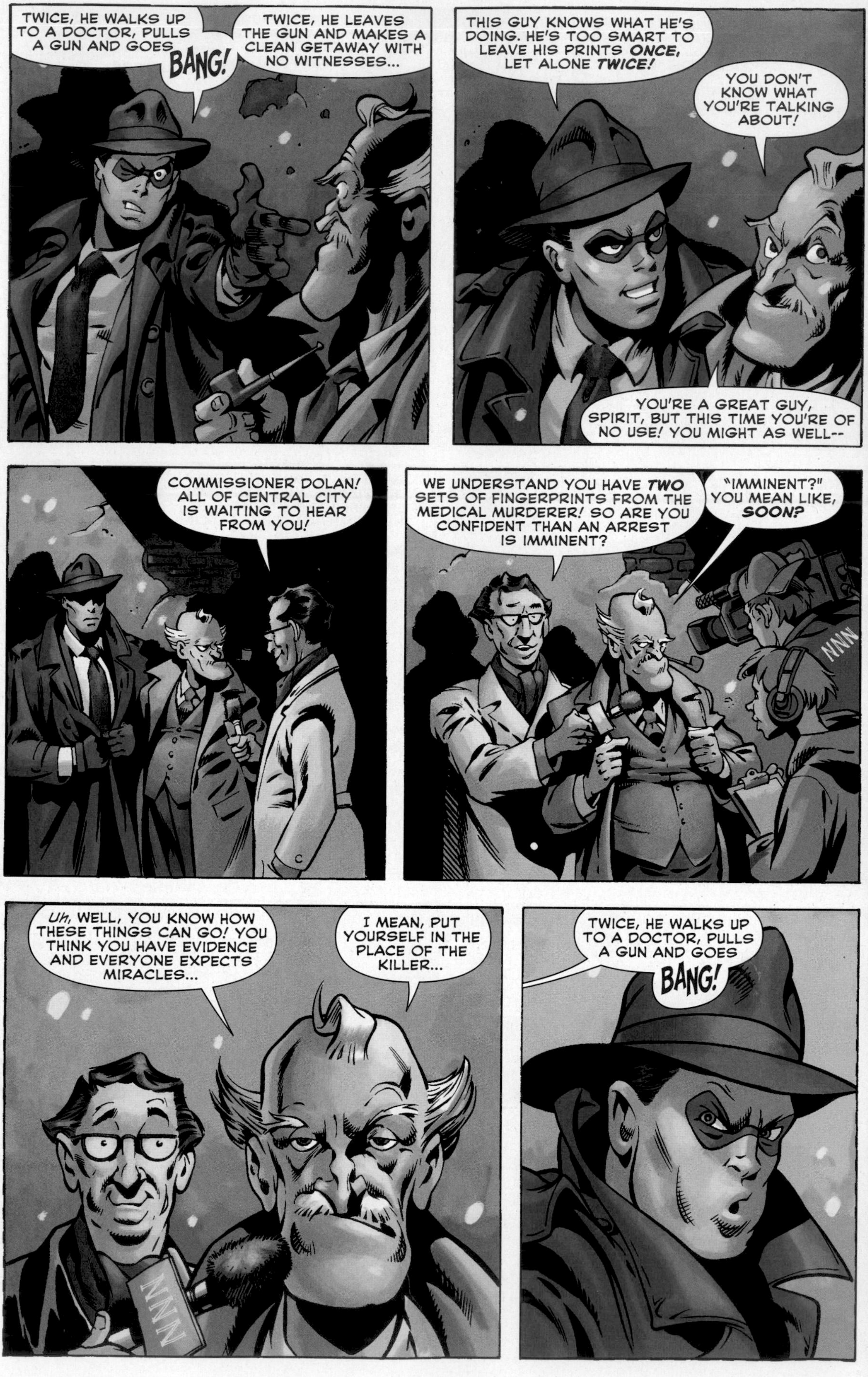
TWICE, HE WALKS UP TO A DOCTOR, PULLS A GUN AND GOES
BANG!
TWICE, HE LEAVES THE GUN AND MAKES A CLEAN GETAWAY WITH NO WITNESSES...
THIS GUY KNOWS WHAT HE'S DOING. HE'S TOO SMART TO LEAVE HIS PRINTS ONCE, LET ALONE TWICE!
YOU DON'T KNOW WHAT YOU'RE TALKING ABOUT!
YOU'RE A GREAT GUY, SPIRIT, BUT THIS TIME YOU'RE OF NO USE! YOU MIGHT AS WELL--
COMMISSIONER DOLAN! ALL OF CENTRAL CITY IS WAITING TO HEAR FROM YOU!
WE UNDERSTAND YOU HAVE TWO SETS OF FINGERPRINTS FROM THE MEDICAL MURDERER! SO ARE YOU CONFIDENT THAN AN ARREST IS IMMINENT?
"IMMINENT?" YOU MEAN LIKE, SOON?
NNN
UH, WELL, YOU KNOW HOW THESE THINGS CAN GO! YOU THINK YOU HAVE EVIDENCE AND EVERYONE EXPECTS MIRACLES...
I MEAN, PUT YOURSELF IN THE PLACE OF THE KILLER...
NNN
TWICE, HE WALKS UP TO A DOCTOR, PULLS A GUN AND GOES
BANG!

Before long...

ANY NEWS?

ANY MINUTE NOW. BUT YOU'LL SEE. THOSE PRINTS WILL LEAD US RIGHT TO THE KILLER. I FEEL IT IN MY GUT.

POLICE HQ

COMMISSIONER! THE LAB WAS ABLE TO LIFT A CLEAN SET OF PRINTS OFF EACH OF THE MURDER WEAPONS.

WHAT DID I TELL YOU?

WHOSE ARE THEY?

WELL, WE HAD A LITTLE TROUBLE THERE. WE DIDN'T FIND A MATCH IN THE INTEGRATED AUTOMATED FINGERPRINT IDENTIFICATION SYSTEM...

DID YOU TRY MILITARY RECORDS?

I DID...AND I FOUND A MATCH TO A SAMUEL HOTCHKISS-- A RATHER HIGHLY DECORATED WAR VETERAN!

WHICH WAR? IRAQ? PERSIAN GULF? GRENADA? VIETNAM?

THE BIG ONE--WORLD WAR II! "BORN: AUGUST 3, 1911... ENTERED SERVICE: MAY 2, 1929... DISCHARGED: APRIL 22, 1947."

I HAVE AN ADDRESS.

BORN IN 1911? THAT WOULD MAKE HIM...

uh...

97 YEARS OLD.

WHO'S 97 YEARS OLD? DAD, HAVE YOU BEEN LYING ABOUT YOUR AGE TO ME?

I'M BUSY, ELLEN. I'M TRYING TO FIGURE OUT WHY A 97-YEAR-OLD MAN WOULD MURDER TWO DOCTORS.

MAYBE THEY CUT OFF HIS SUPPLY OF VIAGRA.

Oh, HI, SPIRIT!

I NEVER COULD HIDE FROM YOU.

HERE'S WHERE MR. HOTCHKISS LIVES-- THE SHADY GLEN ASSISTED LIVING FACILITY.

THE OLD FOLKS' HOME. AND YOU SAY BOTH SETS OF PRINTS WERE A PERFECT MATCH?

NO, JUST YESTERDAY'S. TODAY'S MURDER WEAPON HAS THE PRINTS OF A MRS. SYLVIA BERKOWITZ, ALSO A SHADY GLEN RESIDENT.

OF COURSE, SHE'S A MUCH YOUNGER WOMAN...

...SHE'S 83!

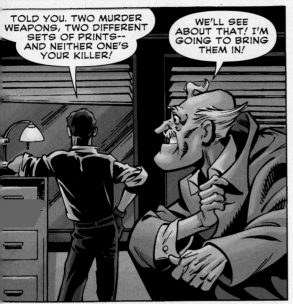

TOLD YOU. TWO MURDER WEAPONS, TWO DIFFERENT SETS OF PRINTS-- AND NEITHER ONE'S YOUR KILLER!

WE'LL SEE ABOUT THAT! I'M GOING TO BRING THEM IN!

WHO LET *YOU* IN HERE?

DO YOU HAVE A STATEMENT, COMMISSIONER? HOW SOON CAN WE EXPECT AN ARREST IN THE MEDICAL MURDERER MYSTERY?

PERHAPS *TONIGHT?* WE'RE AIRING A SPECIAL ON IT...

WHEN WE HAVE SOMETHING, WE'LL TELL YOU!

JUST TELL US THIS. DO YOU HAVE A SUSPECT?

YES, AND I HAVE TO GET TO THEM IN A HURRY...

...BECAUSE THEY MAY NOT LIVE THROUGH THE INTERROGATION!

97 YEARS OLD! IF YOU'RE GOING TO KILL, THAT'S THE TIME! WHAT WOULD A LIFE SENTENCE BE LIKE? A COUPLE WEEKS?

I WANT TO GO TO THE HOME OF YESTERDAY'S VICTIM, THIS DR. GRIFFEE! I HAVE THE ADDRESS.

SURE I COULDN'T INTEREST YOU IN GETTING THERE BY WAY OF VITO'S?

MAYBE LATER. I WANT TO SEE IF THERE'S ANY CONNECTION BETWEEN THE TWO DOCTORS BESIDES PROFESSION!

HEAD OVER TO PARKVIEW CIRCLE...AND NO PIZZA DETOURS!

WHATEVER YOU SAY.

≷SIGH!≷

Fourteen minutes later...

NO... NO REASON WHY ANYONE WOULD WANT TO KILL HIM! HE DIDN'T HAVE AN ENEMY IN THE WORLD...

THIS PICTURE YOU HAD ON THE MANTLE, MRS. STERNBOTTOM... IS THAT HIM?

HIM AND HIS COLLEGE BUDDIES! THEIR FRATERNITY HAD THE TOP ROWING TEAM! ALL HIS TROPHIES ARE UPSTAIRS...

THAT'S AL THERE. THIS IS YEARS BEFORE I MET HIM, BUT HE WAS SO HANDSOME THEN. THE OTHERS ARE FLETCHER, HARRY AND GRIFF!

"GRIFF"? THAT WOULDN'T BE A NICKNAME FOR GRIFFEE, WOULD IT?

YES, JOE GRIFFEE. OR I GUESS I SHOULD SAY *DOCTOR* JOE GRIFFEE. HE FIXED MY FEET UP SO WELL. YOU CAN TAKE THAT IF YOU LIKE.

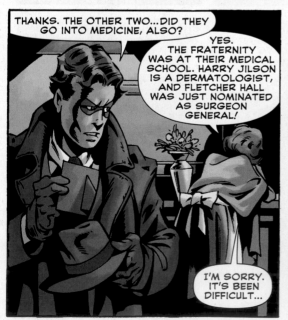

THANKS. THE OTHER TWO...DID THEY GO INTO MEDICINE, ALSO?

YES. THE FRATERNITY WAS AT THEIR MEDICAL SCHOOL. HARRY JILSON IS A DERMATOLOGIST, AND FLETCHER HALL WAS JUST NOMINATED AS SURGEON GENERAL!

I'M SORRY. IT'S BEEN DIFFICULT...

I UNDERSTAND. I'M SORRY FOR YOUR LOSS, MA'AM. I CAN'T BRING HIM BACK, BUT I THINK I CAN FIND THE MAN WHO DID IT.

IF YOU CAN, FINE. LIKE YOU SAID, IT WON'T BRING AL BACK.

I THINK PIZZA'S GOING TO HAVE TO WAIT A LITTLE LONGER.

I FIGURED AS MUCH. YOU WANT TO GO VISIT THE HOME OF THE DOCTOR WHO WAS KILLED YESTERDAY?

NO... ONE OF TWO OTHERS MAY BE IN DANGER!

STOP HERE AT THE NEWSPAPER!

YOU CAN GO GET YOUR PIZZA BECAUSE THIS WILL TAKE A WHILE! I NEED TO SIFT THROUGH THE ARCHIVES AND LOOK UP AN OLD ROWING TEAM!

THAT'S THE *HARD WAY* TO DO IT!

REALLY? WHAT'S THE EASY WAY?

SEARCH ENGINES. WHEN YOU HAVE A WI-FI CARD IN YOUR LAPTOP, THE INFO COMES TO YOU!

SO WHAT AM I LOOKING FOR?

THIS PHOTO... IT'S THE ROWING TEAM FROM A FRAT CALLED PHI KAPPA PSI AT ELMWOOD MEDICAL TECH, CLASS OF '69.

SLOW IT DOWN! I CAN'T TYPE THAT FAST, ESPECIALLY IN HERE!

THERE'S A WHOLE MESS OF STORIES HERE! THIS ONE'S ABOUT AN INVESTIGATION OF SOME SORT...

THAT'S IT! THAT'S WHAT I'M LOOKING FOR!

GOOD WORK! DOLAN'S GOING TO BE SO HAPPY WHEN I WRAP THIS ONE UP!

HOW HAPPY?

NO STOPPING OR PARKING

I MEAN, LIKE, HAPPY ENOUGH TO GET A TICKET FIXED? I HOPE HE'S AT LEAST *THAT* HAPPY!

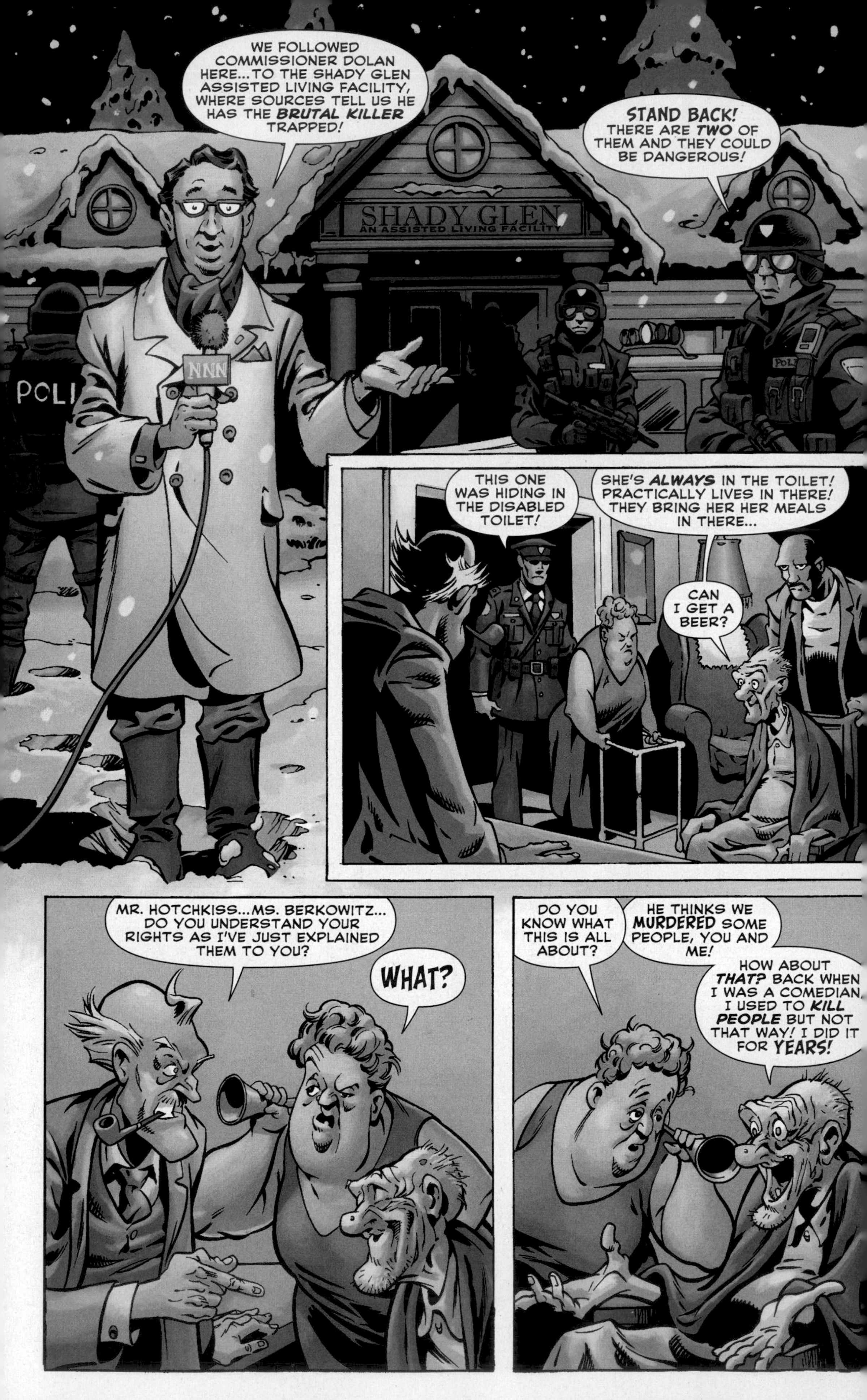
WE FOLLOWED COMMISSIONER DOLAN HERE...TO THE SHADY GLEN ASSISTED LIVING FACILITY, WHERE SOURCES TELL US HE HAS THE BRUTAL KILLER TRAPPED!
SHADY GLEN
AN ASSISTED LIVING FACILITY
NNN
POLI
STAND BACK! THERE ARE TWO OF THEM AND THEY COULD BE DANGEROUS!
THIS ONE WAS HIDING IN THE DISABLED TOILET!
SHE'S ALWAYS IN THE TOILET! PRACTICALLY LIVES IN THERE! THEY BRING HER HER MEALS IN THERE...
CAN I GET A BEER?
MR. HOTCHKISS...MS. BERKOWITZ... DO YOU UNDERSTAND YOUR RIGHTS AS I'VE JUST EXPLAINED THEM TO YOU?
WHAT?
DO YOU KNOW WHAT THIS IS ALL ABOUT?
HE THINKS WE MURDERED SOME PEOPLE, YOU AND ME!
HOW ABOUT THAT? BACK WHEN I WAS A COMEDIAN I USED TO KILL PEOPLE BUT NOT THAT WAY! I DID IT FOR YEARS!

HAT ABOUT *BEERS?* WHAT DID OU DO FOR *BEERS?*

NOT *BEERS,* YOU OLD BAT! *YEARS!* DID I EVER DO MY ACT FOR YOU?

EVERY DAY SINCE I TURNED SEVENTY! HEY, WHO'S THE GEEZER WITH THE PIPE?

I BOUGHT A SUIT WITH TWO PAIR OF PANTS! BUT IT'S BEEN TOO WARM LATELY TO WEAR BOTH PAIR!

WILL YOU TWO *SHUT UP?* I NEED TO QUESTION YOU IN CONNECTION WITH TWO MURDERS!

GIRDERS? WHAT ABOUT GIRDERS?

ONLY TIME I WEAR BOTH PAIR IS WHEN I PLAY GOLF! THAT'S IN CASE I GET A HOLE IN ONE!

WHAT'S THERE A HOLE IN?

HEY, I KNOW WHO THIS GUY REMINDS ME OF! BOBO BERENDO, THE AUSTRALIAN VENTRILOQUIST!

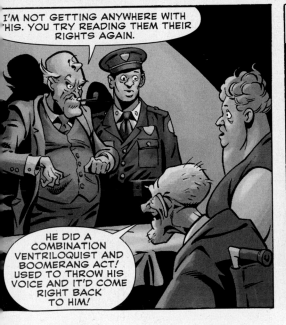

I'M NOT GETTING ANYWHERE WITH THIS. YOU TRY READING THEM THEIR RIGHTS AGAIN.

HE DID A COMBINATION VENTRILOQUIST AND BOOMERANG ACT! USED TO THROW HIS VOICE AND IT'D COME RIGHT BACK TO HIM!

YOU HAVE THE RIGHT TO REMAIN SILENT...

WHAT?

BOBO AND I USED TO PLAY THE MERIDIAN HOTEL UP IN THE CATSKILLS. IT WAS HIM, ME, MARIO LANZA AND A BEAR ACT.

CAN I GET A BEER?

TOSS 'EM IN THE LOCKUP UNTIL THEY CAN EXPLAIN HOW THEIR PRINTS WERE ON THE MURDER WEAPONS.

I HOPE THAT INTERVIEW WILL HELP!

IT WILL. I'M JUST GOING TO TAPE A TAG FOR IT NOW...

THAT WAS ELLEN DOLAN, DAUGHTER OF OUR POLICE COMMISSIONER, EXPRESSING TOTAL CONFIDENCE IN HER FATHER...

HE HAS TWO SUSPECTS IN CUSTODY WHO AT THIS VERY MOMENT ARE BEING TRANSPORTED TO THE COUNTY GENERAL JAIL...

I DID THE *ED SULLIVAN SHOW* EIGHT TIMES. THE MAN NEVER ONCE GOT MY NAME RIGHT...

...KEPT INTRODUCING ME AS TRINI LOPEZ...

...AND THEY CAN **ROT** IN THERE UNTIL I GET SOME ANSWERS!

YOU AGAIN? WHERE ARE YOU OFF TO NOW?

JUST PASSING THROUGH ON MY WAY TO SEE A DOCTOR...

YOU SICK OR SOMETHING?

NO, BUT SOMEONE *ELSE'S* HEALTH MAY BE IN JEOPARDY...

Before long...

I'D LIKE TO SEE DR. JILSON, PLEASE.

I'M AFRAID THE DOCTOR HAD TO LEAVE TOWN UNEXPECTEDLY.

IT LOOKS LIKE IT WAS SO UNEXPECTED THAT HE LEFT WITHOUT HIS LUGGAGE!

Oh, THAT. WELL, uh...

TALK TO ME, JEEVES. YOUR EMPLOYER'S LIFE IS ON THE LINE HERE!

HE SAW THE NEWS REPORT... ABOUT THE SECOND OF HIS FRIENDS FROM COLLEGE BEING MURDERED...

RIGHT. TWO FRIENDS IN TWO DAYS. I'D BE WORRIED, TOO.

HE BOOKED A FLIGHT OUT OF TOWN AND HAD ME PACK HIS BAGS. THEN HE GOT A CALL...

...SOMETHING ABOUT AN EMERGENCY CALL TO **SHADY GLEN!** WHOEVER CALLED WANTED HIM THERE TONIGHT AT EIGHT...

HE MOVED TO A LATER FLIGHT, THEN RAN OUT OF HERE WITHOUT HIS LUGGAGE. I DON'T KNOW WHAT TO DO ABOUT HIS APPOINTMENTS!

I DON'T, EITHER... BUT I THINK I'LL BE KEEPING THE ONE AT SHADY GLEN TONIGHT AT EIGHT.

EB? CALL MONA AT THE D.A.'S OFFICE! I NEED A LITTLE **BANKING** INFORMATION! AND YOU KEEP GOOGLING THOSE GUYS IN THE FRATERNITY!

SHADY GLEN
AN ASSISTED LIVING FACILITY

BUT FIRST, COME PICK ME UP AND TAKE ME TO AN APPOINTMENT...

That night, just after eight...

...an unknown figure, strolling into Shady Glen...

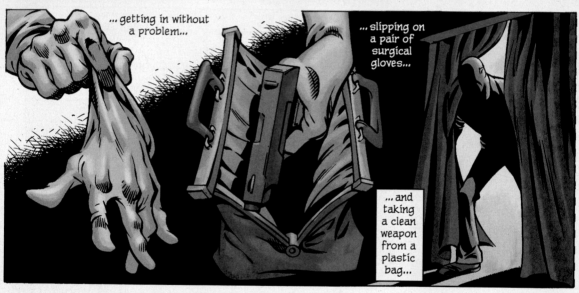

...getting in without a problem...

...slipping on a pair of surgical gloves...

...and taking a clean weapon from a plastic bag...

DOESN'T MATTER WHICH ONE I PICK! THIS OLD GUY HERE IN THE HALLWAY IS AS GOOD A CHOICE AS ANY...

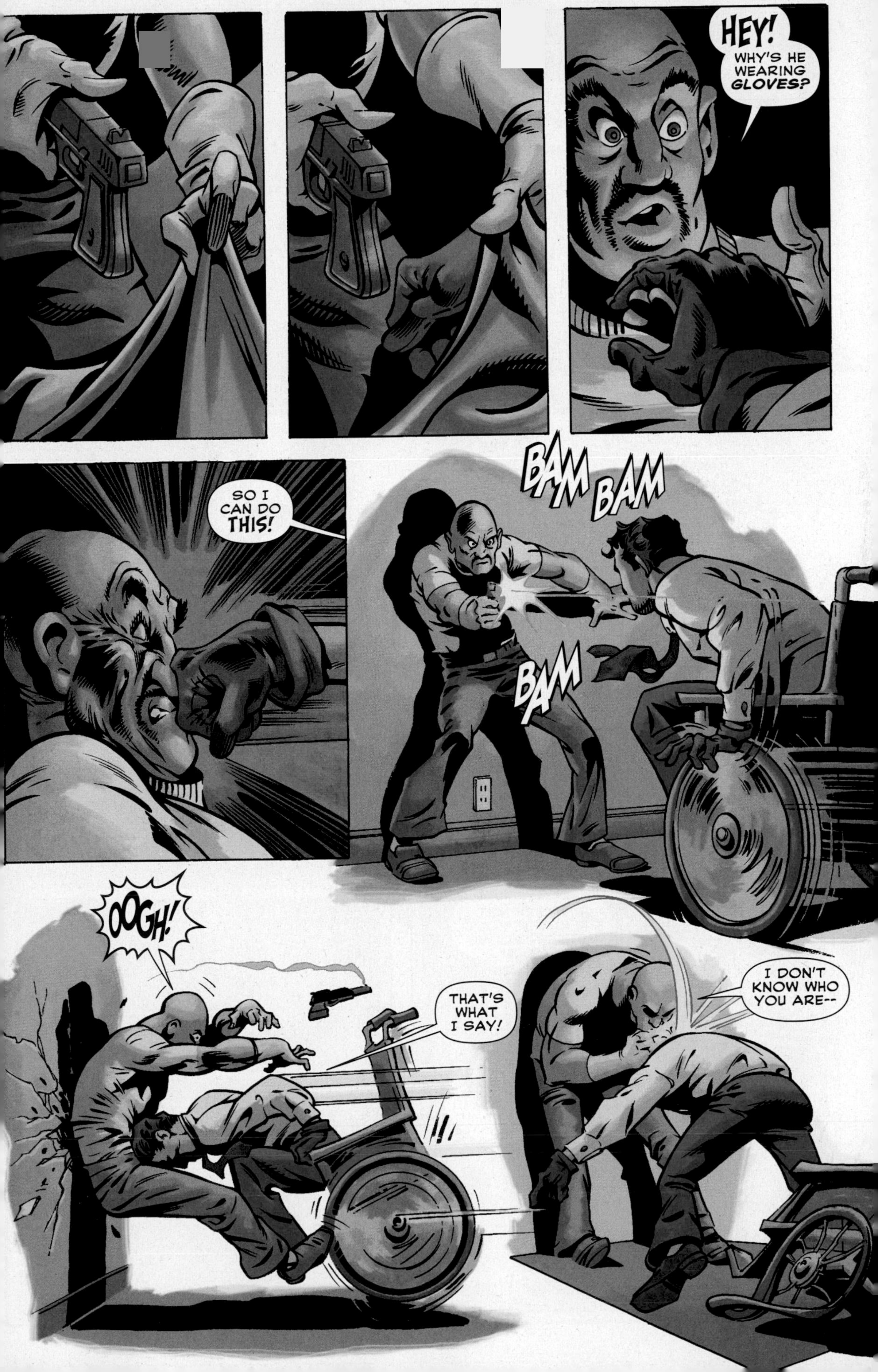
HEY! WHY'S HE WEARING GLOVES?
SO I CAN DO THIS!
BAM BAM
BAM
OOGH!
THAT'S WHAT I SAY!
I DON'T KNOW WHO YOU ARE--

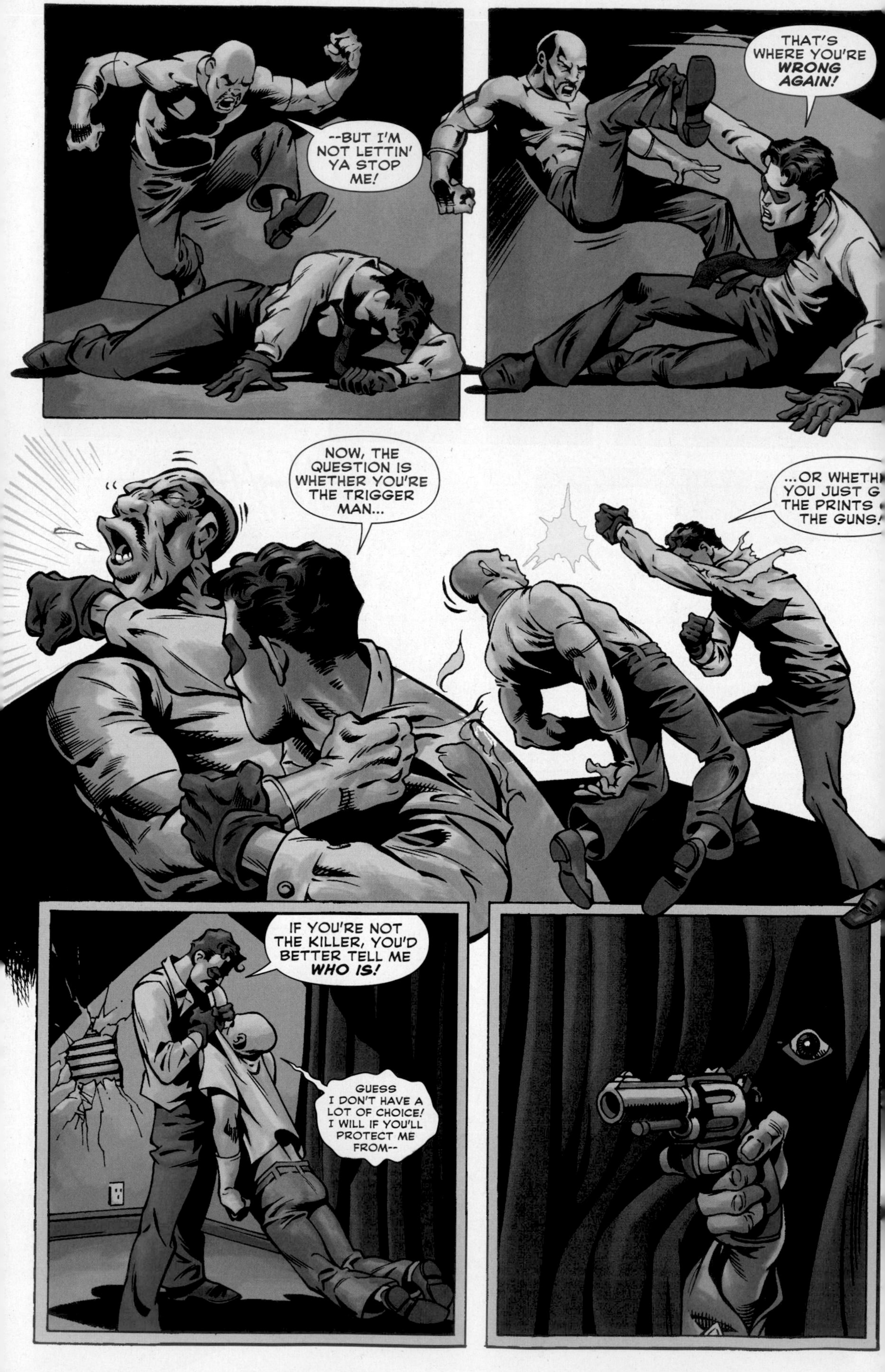
--BUT I'M NOT LETTIN' YA STOP ME!
THAT'S WHERE YOU'RE *WRONG AGAIN!*
NOW, THE QUESTION IS WHETHER YOU'RE THE TRIGGER MAN...
...OR WHETH YOU JUST G THE PRINTS THE GUNS!
IF YOU'RE NOT THE KILLER, YOU'D BETTER TELL ME *WHO IS!*
GUESS I DON'T HAVE A LOT OF CHOICE! I WILL IF YOU'LL PROTECT ME FROM--

NGBANG
ANG
NG

BANG BANG

--FROM THAT, I GUESS!

THIS IS PROBABLY A WASTE OF TIME, BUT I HAVE TO GO LOOK--!

YEP. WASTE OF TIME.

BUT AT LEAST I KNOW THERE IS SOMEONE ELSE FIRING THE GUNS!

EB? CALL THE COPS! TELL 'EM I HAVE A DEAD BODY HERE FOR THEM!

NO, IT'S NOT THE DERMATOLOGIST! I'LL EXPLAIN WHEN YOU COME GET ME...

...AND NO, WE'RE NOT STOPPING AT VITO'S.

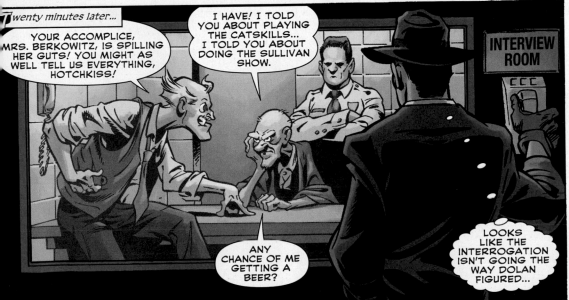

Twenty minutes later...

YOUR ACCOMPLICE, MRS. BERKOWITZ, IS SPILLING HER GUTS! YOU MIGHT AS WELL TELL US EVERYTHING, HOTCHKISS!

I HAVE! I TOLD YOU ABOUT PLAYING THE CATSKILLS... I TOLD YOU ABOUT DOING THE SULLIVAN SHOW.

INTERVIEW ROOM

ANY CHANCE OF ME GETTING A BEER?

LOOKS LIKE THE INTERROGATION ISN'T GOING THE WAY DOLAN FIGURED...

SPIRIT, CAN YOU JUST *BUTT OUT?* I HAVE THIS CASE LOCKED UP! I AM *THIS CLOSE* TO GETTING THEM TO CONFESS!

ALL RIGHT, ALL RIGHT! I *CONFESS!* I STOLE HALF MY ACT FROM JACKIE MASON! CAN I GO BACK TO SHADY GLEN NOW? IT'S TURKEY MEATLOAF NIGHT!

GET YOUR TUX AND MEET ME AT THE MARRIOTT OUT BY THE AIRPORT!

NO, YOU DON'T HAVE TO GO...BUT IF YOU DON'T, I'LL BE WRAPPING UP THE CASE WITHOUT YOU!

And so...

SIR, THERE'S NO SMOKING IN THE BALLROOM!

YES, AND THERE'S NO TOBACCO IN THE PIPE! HASN'T BEEN ANY IN YEARS!

WE'RE JUST IN TIME! THEY'RE ABOUT TO INTRODUCE THE NEW SURGEON GENERAL DESIGNATE...

...AND LOOK WHO'S DOING THE INTRODUCTION! YOUR OLD FRIEND!

NOT *HIM* AGAIN!

...SUCH AN HONOR TO INTRODUCE SUCH A *SUCCESSFUL* MAN, WHO WILL SOON BE SERVING US IN WASHINGTON... DOCTOR FLETCHER HALL!

THANK YOU...

I WON'T ACTUALLY *BE* YOUR SURGEON GENERAL UNTIL THE SENATE CONFIRMS ME NEXT WEEK, BUT--

SORRY... I DON'T THINK THAT'S GOING TO HAPPEN!

WHAT IS *THIS* ALL ABOUT?

IT'S ABOUT SOMETHING THAT HAPPENED A LONG TIME AGO...AN INCIDENT ON A LAKE, DR. PECK. **REMEMBER?**

IT'S A LIE!

WHOEVER TOLD YOU THAT, IT'S A LIE! THIS IS ALL A CHEAP TRICK TO DENY ME MY RIGHTFUL POSITION!

WE CHECKED YOUR BANK ACCOUNTS AND THOSE OF YOUR FORMER FRAT BROTHERS! YOU'RE UNDER ARREST FOR KILLING TWO OF THEM!

TAKE HIM IN!

YOU CAN'T PROVE A THING! I'LL SUE THE CITY! I'LL SUE **YOU,** PERSONALLY! I'LL--

THE GUY YOU HIRED TO PUT THE OLD FOLKS' PRINTS ON THE GUN-- HE TOLD THE SPIRIT...

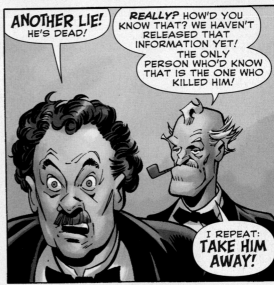

ANOTHER LIE! HE'S DEAD!

REALLY? HOW'D YOU KNOW THAT? WE HAVEN'T RELEASED THAT INFORMATION YET! THE ONLY PERSON WHO'D KNOW THAT IS THE ONE WHO KILLED HIM!

I REPEAT: **TAKE HIM AWAY!**

NICE WORK, COMMISH! BUT HOW DID ARRESTING THOSE **OLD FOLKS** HELP YOU BUST THE CASE OPEN?

OH, **THEM?** THEY WERE, uh...

THEY WERE **RED HERRINGS--** YOU KNOW, TO THROW THE REAL KILLER OFF, MAKE HIM THINK WE WEREN'T LOOKING FOR HIM WHEN WE WERE...

I HAVE TO GO...

SPIRIT, CAN YOU GIVE ME A LIFT BACK TO SHADY GLEN? I'LL CALL AND HAVE MY "SUSPECTS" RETURNED THERE...

EBONY'S WAITING OUTSIDE.

SO... HOW'D YOU PUT TWO AND TWO TOGETHER ON THIS?

I FOUND AN OLD ARTICLE ON THE 'NET ABOUT THEIR TEAM AND THIS LAKE THEY COMPETED ON...

...AND ANOTHER ONE ABOUT THIS GIRL BEING FOUND DEAD IN THE LAKE! NO ONE EVER KNEW HOW OR WHY!

THE SPIRIT WAS THE ONE WHO REALLY DID THE MATH...FIGURED THEY WERE CONNECTED, GUESSED THAT MAYBE THE THREE OF THEM WERE BLACKMAILING THEIR OLD PAL!

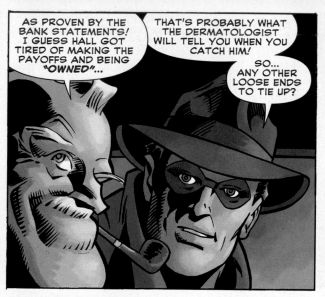

AS PROVEN BY THE BANK STATEMENTS! I GUESS HALL GOT TIRED OF MAKING THE PAYOFFS AND BEING *"OWNED"*...

THAT'S PROBABLY WHAT THE DERMATOLOGIST WILL TELL YOU WHEN YOU CATCH HIM!

SO... ANY OTHER LOOSE ENDS TO TIE UP?

JUST *ONE!* EB, COULD YOU STOP AT THIS FLORIST SHOP FOR A SEC?

SURE THING, COMMISSIONER!

FLOWERS

TAXI!

*S*oon...

ELLEN! WHAT ARE YOU DOING HERE?

I HITCHED A RIDE IN THE WAGON THAT BROUGHT MR. HOTCHKISS AND MRS. BERKOWITZ BACK HOME!

AND JUST IN TIME! IT'S TURKEY MEATLOAF NIGHT!

I'M AFRAID SOME OF US HAVE TO EAT SOME *CROW* INSTEAD!

MRS. BERKOWITZ...MR. HOTCHKISS... I'VE COME TO APOLOGIZE FOR THE WAY I-- THAT IS, *THE POLICE* DETAINED YOU LIKE THAT.

WHAT?

HE'S EMBARRASSED AND HUMILIATED AND HE BROUGHT US FLOWERS! I HATE FLOWERS!

Ah, BUT FOR *YOU*, MR. HOTCHKISS, I BROUGHT SOMETHING *BETTER*...

OLD HEN BEER

THE REASON I CAME HERE, DADDY, IS TO LOOK AROUND! IT REALLY IS A LOVELY PLACE!

THAT'S NICE, BUT WHY WOULD *YOU* BE INTERESTED IN THAT?

YOUR DAUGHTER IS QUITE CONSCIENTIOUS, COMMISSIONER! SHE THINKS ONE OF OUR MID-SIZED ROOMS WILL SUIT YOU! WE SHOULD HAVE ONE AVAILABLE IN JUST A FEW WEEKS!

SPIRIT! WANT TO LEAVE *NOW!*

"...JUST A FEW WEEKS..." THE NERVE...

BUT DADDY, WE HAVE TO PLAN FOR THE FUTURE...

THE END

Art by Bruce Timm & Dave Stewart

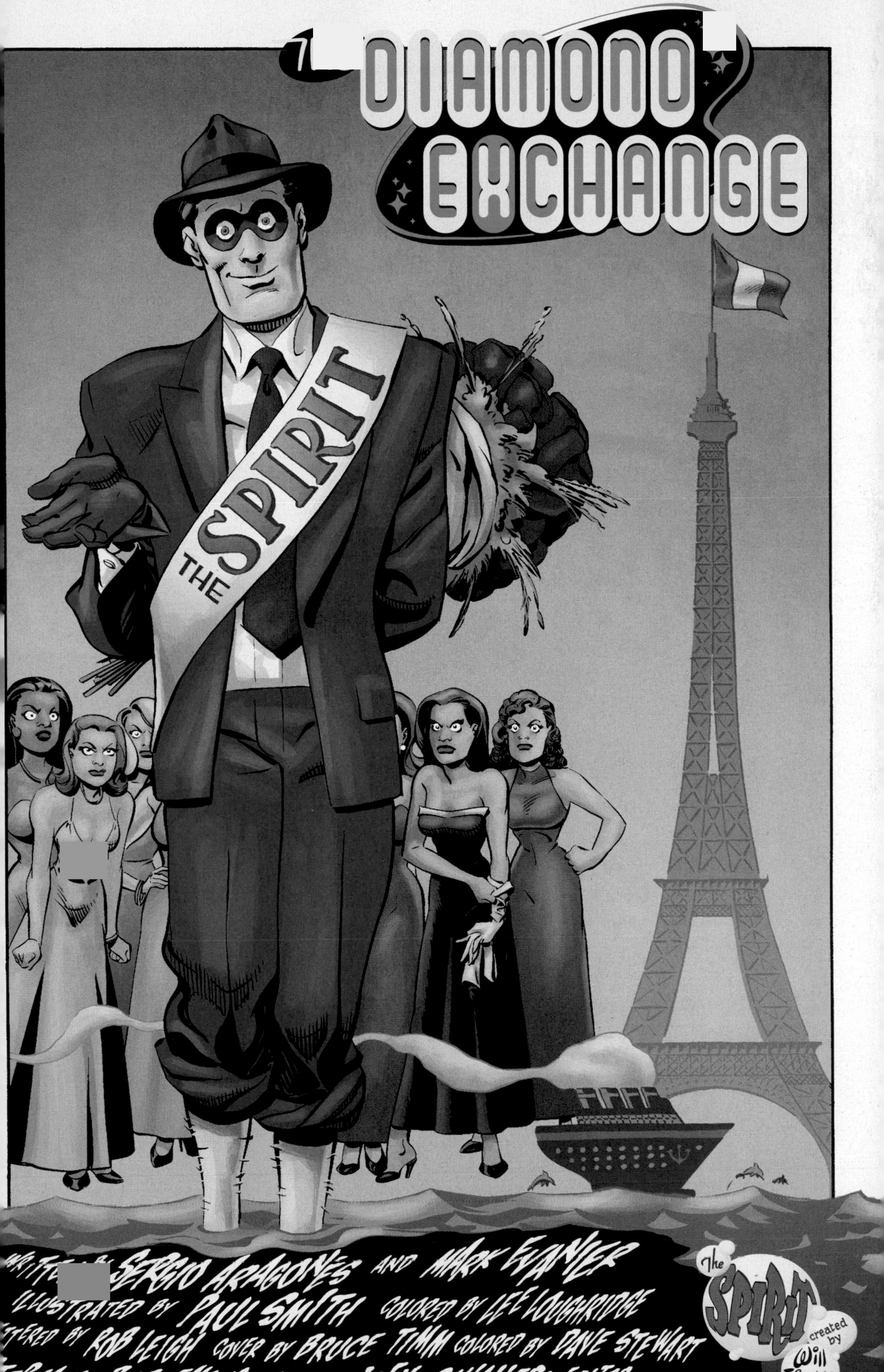
DIAMOND EXCHANGE
THE SPIRIT
SERGIO ARAGONÉS AND MARK EVANIER
ILLUSTRATED BY PAUL SMITH COLORED BY LEE LOUGHRIDGE
TTERED BY ROB LEIGH COVER BY BRUCE TIMM COLORED BY DAVE STEWART
EPHANIE BUSCEMA, ASST. EDITOR JOEY CAVALIERI, EDITOR
The SPIRIT created by Will Eisner

Funny thing about waiting in the cab line: You never know who's going to get in...

...could be a tourist... could be a professional woman... could be a big-tipping big business man...

...could even be a guy with two slugs in his gut...

I'M IN LUCK! THAT'S *EBONY'S* CAB...

WHO AM I KIDDING? I'M NOT GONNA MAKE IT... GOTTA BE TWENTY BLOCKS TO THE HOSPITAL...

EBONY...

BEEN OUT DRINKING ALL NIGHT AGAIN, SAM? YOU'VE GOTTA--

OH, *JEEZ!* WHAT HAPPENED TO *YOU?*

I TOLD A FENCE I WAS GOIN' TO THE COPS TO TURN STATE'S EVIDENCE! NOT A BRIGHT THING TO DO...

DOESN'T LOOK THAT WAY! I'LL GET YOU TO AN EMERGENCY ROOM AND--

SAVE YOUR GAS!

HEY, WHAT'S THE BIGGEST TIP YOU EVER GOT, EBONY? ANYONE EVER TIP YOU IN *DIAMONDS?*

TAKE 'EM! LOUSY FENCE DOESN'T WANT 'EM! *NOBODY* WANTS 'EM!

JUST HOLD ON, SAM! I'M CALLING *911!*

THEY'RE ALL SAVIN' THEIR MONEY FOR THE BIG SHIPMENT...

LOOK HOW THEY *SPARKLE,* EBONY! EVERYTHING

SPARKLES...

EVERYTHING...

Slow fade to black.

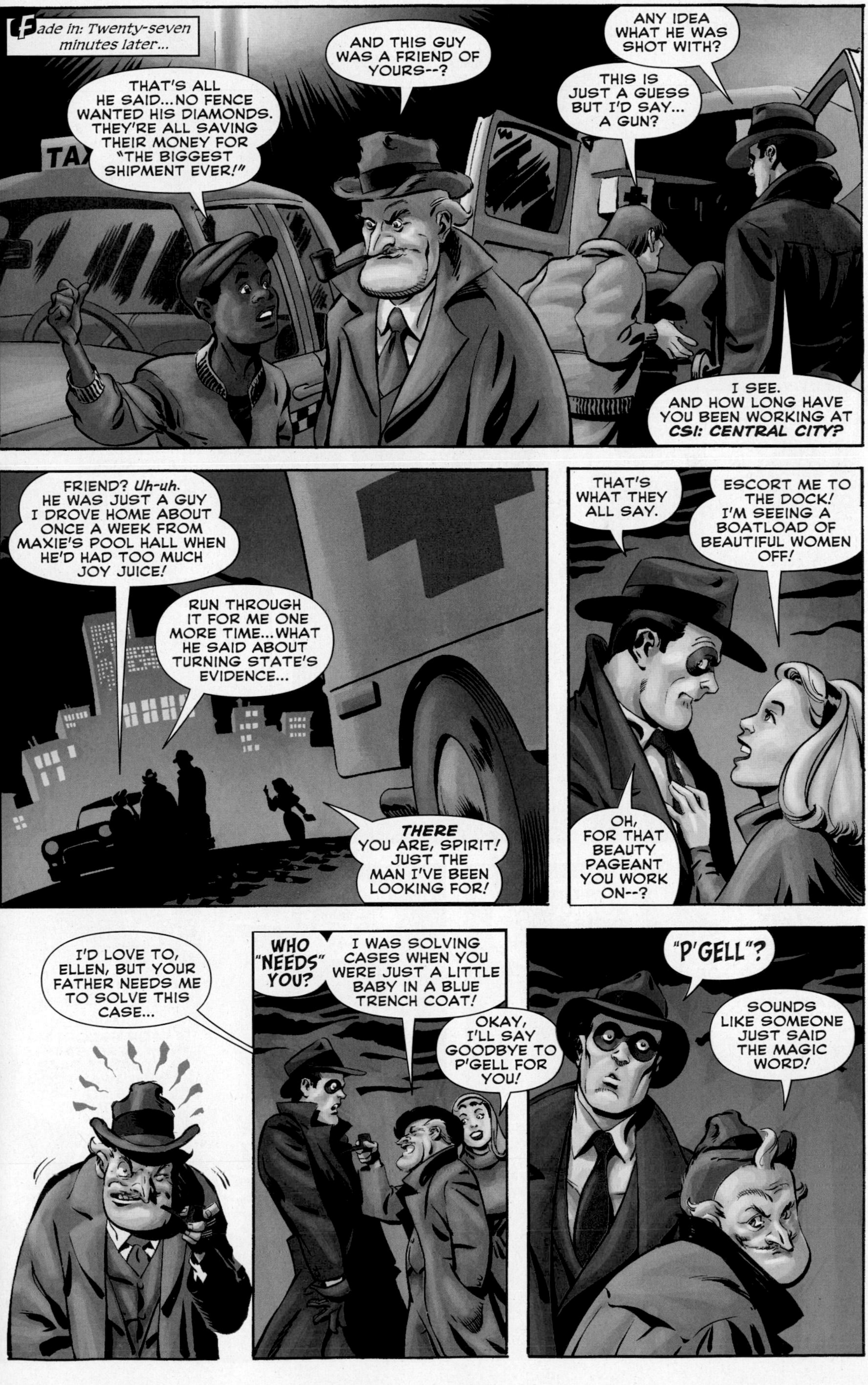
Fade in: Twenty-seven minutes later...
THAT'S ALL HE SAID...NO FENCE WANTED HIS DIAMONDS. THEY'RE ALL SAVING THEIR MONEY FOR "THE BIGGEST SHIPMENT EVER!"
TAX
AND THIS GUY WAS A FRIEND OF YOURS--?
ANY IDEA WHAT HE WAS SHOT WITH?
THIS IS JUST A GUESS BUT I'D SAY... A GUN?
I SEE. AND HOW LONG HAVE YOU BEEN WORKING AT CSI: CENTRAL CITY?
FRIEND? Uh-uh. HE WAS JUST A GUY I DROVE HOME ABOUT ONCE A WEEK FROM MAXIE'S POOL HALL WHEN HE'D HAD TOO MUCH JOY JUICE!
RUN THROUGH IT FOR ME ONE MORE TIME...WHAT HE SAID ABOUT TURNING STATE'S EVIDENCE...
THERE YOU ARE, SPIRIT! JUST THE MAN I'VE BEEN LOOKING FOR!
THAT'S WHAT THEY ALL SAY.
ESCORT ME TO THE DOCK! I'M SEEING A BOATLOAD OF BEAUTIFUL WOMEN OFF!
OH, FOR THAT BEAUTY PAGEANT YOU WORK ON--?
I'D LOVE TO, ELLEN, BUT YOUR FATHER NEEDS ME TO SOLVE THIS CASE...
WHO "NEEDS" YOU?
I WAS SOLVING CASES WHEN YOU WERE JUST A LITTLE BABY IN A BLUE TRENCH COAT!
OKAY, I'LL SAY GOODBYE TO P'GELL FOR YOU!
"P'GELL"?
SOUNDS LIKE SOMEONE JUST SAID THE MAGIC WORD!

Each year, the Ms. World Supermodel competition is held in a different city. This year, Paris is playing host...

SURE YOU WON'T SAIL WITH US, SPIRIT? FRANCE IS BEAUTIFUL THIS TIME OF YEAR...

...AND SO AM I.

YES, YOU ARE. BUT I'M AFRAID I'M NEEDED HERE TO HANDLE A MATTER OF SOME IMPORTANCE!

AHEM!

YOU HEARD THE MAN. BESIDES, HE'S *MY* ESCORT! AREN'T YOU, SPIRIT, DEAR?

Oh, RIGHT. WHAT SHE SAID!

ELLEN! THANK YOU FOR ALL YOU AND THE COMMITTEE HAVE DONE FOR ME! I PROMISE TO BRING BACK THE TITLE OF MS. WORLD SUPERMODEL!

I'LL BE WITH YOU IN A SECOND, LYDIA! I HAVE TO CHAPERONE ONE OF YOUR CHAPERONES!

I KNOW WHAT YOU'RE THINKING: WHAT'S IN IT FOR ME?

WHY HAVE I SIGNED ON AS A CHAPERONE FOR A BOATLOAD OF BEAUTY PAGEANT CONTESTANTS?

THERE'S GOT TO BE AN ANGLE. I KNOW YOU TOO WELL, P'GELL!

P'GELL! THE SHIP IS ABOUT TO SAIL!

Ah, BUT NOT AS WELL AS BOTH OF US WOULD LIKE!

THANK YOU FOR ESCORTING ME HERE, SPIRIT! I WON'T TAKE YOU AWAY FROM KISSING THAT WOMAN!

ELLEN, *WAIT!*

I WASN'T KISSING HER! *SHE* WAS KISSING *ME!*

WHERE TO, LADY?

SOMEWHERE MEN DON'T WEAR MASKS.

SHE'LL FORGIVE ME. MAYBE NOT IN THIS CENTURY BUT SHE'LL FORGIVE ME.

SO...SINCE I'M IN THIS AREA, MAYBE I OUGHTA PAY A VISIT TO FENSTER...SEE WHAT HE KNOWS ABOUT A BIG DIAMOND SHIPMENT...

Fenster runs the Seaside Collateral Finance Service (i.e., a pawn shop by the docks)...

SPIRIT! I DON'T KNOW NOTHIN' ABOUT ANY DIAMONDS!

ODD THAT YOU SHOULD SAY THAT, FENSTER, BECAUSE I HAVEN'T *ASKED* ABOUT ANY DIAMONDS!

Uh, I THOUGHT... WHY WAIT 'TIL THE LAST MINUTE?

YOU KNOW SOMETHING AND I'M NOT LEAVING UNTIL I HEAR!

YOU'RE LEAVIN' *NOW,* PAL...

POINT THAT AWAY FROM ME.

BLAMM

ANYONE EVER TELL YOU YOU'RE NOT A GOOD HOST?

NOW THEN! YOU WERE SAYING ABOUT THAT SHIPMENT...

LOOK, ALL I KNOW IS THAT A SHIPMENT'S COMING! SOMETHING REALLY BIG, THEY SAY! I DON'T KNOW WHEN, I DON'T KNOW HOW...

UNFORTUNATELY, I BELIEVE YOU...

OKAY, SQUARE ONE. BUT IF A SMALL-TIMER LIKE FENSTER HAS HEARD ABOUT IT, IT'S GOT TO BE *HUGE*...

EBONY? IT'S YOUR FAVORITE FARE! PICK ME UP WHERE YOU DROPPED ME OFF. WE'RE GOING TO GO VISIT SOME DIAMOND IMPORTERS...

All day, all night: The Spirit makes the rounds... and gets zero information to show for it...

HELLO, OMAR.

SPIRIT! I HAVE NO INFORMATION FOR YOU!

SORRY... ALL I KNOW IS THAT BASED ON RECENT PRICE FLUCTUATIONS, SOMETHING IS IN THE WIND...

I'M VERY SORRY, MR. SPIRIT, SIR.

I'M GETTING NOWHERE IN A HURRY.

EVERYONE KNOWS IT'S COMING...NOBODY KNOWS WHEN OR WHERE. THE LESS THEY SEEM TO KNOW, THE BIGGER THE WHOLE DEAL SOUNDS.

YOU GOT ANY OTHER DIAMOND MERCHANTS YOU WANT TO GO SEE?

NO...I THINK MAYBE I'D LIKE A RELAXING GAME OF POOL AT MAXIE'S...

And so...

RACK 'EM UP, MAXIE! AND GIVE ME THE UNBENT CUE!

SPIRIT! WHAT BRINGS YOU HERE?

MY FRIEND SAM TOLD ME THIS WAS A GREAT PLACE TO SHOOT A FEW GAMES. YOU REMEMBER *SAM*...

HE TOLD ME A *LOT* OF THINGS ABOUT THIS PLACE BEFORE SOMEONE SHOT HIM! AND I THINK YOU KNOW WHODUNNIT, MAXIE...

SAM WAS STUPID TO CROSS THE GUYS WHO SET UP THE FRENCH DEAL!

BUT I'M NOT PLAYING GAMES WITH YOU, SPIRIT...

YOU AREN'T? HERE'S ONE I THINK YOU'LL LIKE...

THREE BALL IN THE CORNER NOSTRIL!

YOU SHOULD TAKE YOUR CUE FROM ME!

GET IT? "TAKE YOUR *CUE*"?

WONDER IF THIS IS THE GUN THAT SHOT SAM...

GOT YOUR BACK!

BOY, THEY USE CHEAP FURNITURE IN THESE PLACES!

I THINK WE NEED TO CALL SOME COPS!

ALREADY DID! MAYBE ONE OF THESE GUYS WILL TALK!

MAYBE. OR MAYBE THE ANSWER HAS BEEN RIGHT IN FRONT OF MY FACE ALL ALONG!

LET'S INTERROGATE THESE GUYS AND SCRAM BEFORE DOLAN'S BOYS GET HERE!

Before long...

I COULD'VE STAYED AND EXPLAINED, BUT THEN I'D HAVE HAD TO DEAL WITH DOLAN! LATELY, HE'S BEEN TRYING TO TURN MY ONE-MAN OPERATION INTO A PARTNERSHIP!

NOW, YOU SAY YOU NEED TICKETS TO *PARIS*, IS IT?

RIGHT. YOU KNOW A TRAVEL AGENCY THAT'S OPEN THIS LATE?

I'M A TRAVEL AGENCY THAT'S OPEN THIS LATE!

WINDOW SEAT OR AISLE?

GREAT. TAKE ME HOME SO I CAN PACK!

JUST AS SOON AS I PRINT YOUR BOARDING PASS!

As the Spirit heads for France, the ship bearing P'Gell and the contestants crosses the Atlantic...

HERE TO DEMONSTRATE THE TALENTS THEY WILL DISPLAY AT THE PAGEANT ARE OUR TOP FINALISTS...

*Hmm...*WHISTLING THE 1812 OVERTURE ON A UNICYCLE...

IT'S TOO GOOD!

LYDIA'S GOT TO WIN! SO WHAT DID HENRI MEAN? "IT'S ALL ARRANGED, BUT YOU'RE BETTER OFF NOT KNOWING HOW!"

...LEAVE A MESSAGE AT THE SOUND OF THE BEEP! *BEEP*

SPIRIT? DOLAN HERE. THIS IS THE **FOURTH** MESSAGE I'VE LEFT FOR YOU!

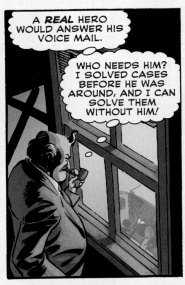

A **REAL** HERO WOULD ANSWER HIS VOICE MAIL.

WHO NEEDS HIM? I SOLVED CASES BEFORE HE WAS AROUND, AND I CAN SOLVE THEM WITHOUT HIM!

I'LL DO SOME LEGWORK... TAP INTO MY SOURCES... FIND OUT ABOUT THIS DIAMOND SHIPMENT MYSELF!

BUT BEFORE I DO, MAYBE I'LL LEAVE A **FIFTH** MESSAGE...

Thousands of miles away...

THERE MAY BE A LITTLE LANGUAGE BARRIER, BUT IT'S SURE A MORE PICTURESQUE PLACE TO LOOK FOR CRIMINALS...

La Maison de Diamond

MONSIEUR VIDAL! I BELIEVE MY FRIEND FROM THE POLICE NATIONALE CONTACTED YOU...

INDEED HE DID, MONSIEUR SPIRIT! HE ASSURED ME I COULD TAKE YOU INTO MY CONFIDENCE AND SO I SHALL!

IT WAS A ROBBERY FROM A SAFE DEPOSIT BOX IN ANTWERP'S DIAMOND EXCHANGE LAST MAY...AN INSIDE JOB, OBVIOUSLY.

THE THIEF OR THIEVES KNEW WHICH BOX TO HIT AND WHEN IT WOULD BE UNGUARDED.

MY FRIEND SAID THE STONES THEY GOT ARE WORTH AT LEAST TEN MILLION DOLLARS! THAT'S MORE THAN 800 MILLION FRANCS.

AT LEAST! I SHALL GATHER TOGETHER SUCH INFORMATION AS WE HAVE. WHERE MIGHT I REACH YOU?

BELIEVE IT OR NOT, YOU MAY BE ABLE TO FIND ME AT A **BEAUTY PAGEANT!**

The following night at the Cite de la Musique Concert Hall...

...THESE TEN FINALISTS WHO HAVE COME FROM ALL ABOUT THE GLOBE TO COMPETE AS MS. WORLD SUPERMODEL!

LYDIA *HAS* TO WIN!

YOU'RE SO NERVOUS, P'GELL, ONE WOULD THINK YOU'RE A CONTESTANT!

SPIRIT! WHY AM I NOT SURPRISED TO SEE YOU HERE OR ANYWHERE?

I'M LIKE THE GUY WHO INSTALLS CABLE TV. YOU NEVER KNOW WHEN I'M GOING TO SHOW UP.

IN THIS CASE, IT'S NOT ODD. BEAUTIFUL WOMEN... JEWELRY...YOU...WHY WOULD A GUY *NOT* BE HERE?

"JEWELRY"?

WELL, YOU CAN BE INTERESTED IN THAT IF YOU LIKE. I'M ONLY INTERESTED IN SEEING MY PROTÉGÉ WIN HERE!

MS. AMERICAN SUPERMODEL? SHE LOOKS LIKE A SHOO-IN!

I AM NOT SURE. MS. SPAIN SUPERMODEL IS GORGEOUS AND PLAYS FLAMENCO GUITAR...

NO, THAT'S BEEN DONE!

...PROBABLY WHILE RIDING A UNICYCLE AND WHISTLING THE 1812 OVERTURE, IF I KNOW BEAUTY PAGEANTS!

THAT NOISE...

THAT LIGHT'S FALLING--

--AND SHE'S RIGHT UNDER IT!

KRASSH!

SORRY, LADY!

¡MI MANO ESTÁ ROTA! YOU BROKE MY HAND! ¡HOMBRE STUPIDO!

HEY, IF NOT FOR ME, THE REST OF YOU WOULD BE BROKEN!

--AND THERE'S THE GUY WHO DID IT!

SIE SIND EIN HELD!

LET ME THROUGH! I HAVE TO GO AFTER SOMEONE!

MEET MY GREAT AMERICAN FRIEND, THE SPIRIT!

ОН НАСТОЛЬКО КРАСИВ!

SMILE, LADIES AND HERO!

COULD I TAKE A RAINCHECK ON ALL THESE HUGS?

IT'S *TOO LATE!* THAT GUY COULD BE IN BELGIUM BY NOW!

THEY DON'T SEEM TO HAVE *ANY* KIND OF SECURITY HERE!

NO ONE'S EVEN GUARDING THIS TIARA!

WHAT IS THE POINT? THE STONES, THEY ARE WORTHLESS GLASS!

ANY IDEA WHO MADE IT?

BUT OF COURSE! MONSIEUR BALISSAT! HE MAKES ALL THE TIARAS!

HE HAS A SHOWROOM TWO BLOCKS DOWN RUE D'AUBERVILLIERS!

THIS IS JUST A HUNCH, BUT IF IT'S RIGHT...

HELLO? MONSIEUR BALISSAT? *ARE YOU HERE?*

I HAVE AN AWFUL FEELING MY HUNCH WAS RIGHT...

YEP.

PROBABLY THE SAME GUY WHO TRIED TO KNOCK MS. SPAIN SUPERMODEL OUT OF THE CONTEST...

HELLO.

ANOTHER TIARA, JUST LIKE THE ONE THAT WILL BE AWARDED TO THE WINNER OF THE PAGEANT...

WHY DO I HAVE THE FEELING THESE DON'T *ALL* HAVE PHONY...?

OW.

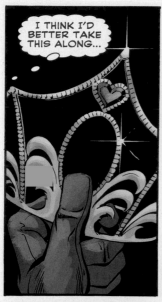

I THINK I'D BETTER TAKE THIS ALONG...

THE PROPRIETOR WON'T MIND, SEEING AS HOW HE'S DEAD AND ALL! I CAN PHONE THE GENDARMES AND TELL THEM...

RIGHT NOW, I'D BETTER GET BACK. THIS IS ALL STARTING TO MAKE TOO MUCH SENSE...

At the auditorium...

WHILE WE AWAIT THE JUDGES' DECISION AND BEFORE WE CROWN OUR WINNER, MS. JAPAN SUPERMODEL WILL ENTERTAIN US WITH HER AMAZING TALENT...

...AND THEN SHE WILL BAKE A BAVARIAN CHOCOLATE PIE!

I HOPE I'M IN TIME...

THE GUY GUARDING THE WINNER'S TIARA IS ASLEEP!

CORRECTION: THE GUY GUARDING THE WINNER'S TIARA IS DEAD!

NO ONE LOOKING...

WONDER WHAT WILL HAPPEN...

...IF WE MAKE A LITTLE *SWITCH*!

IF NOTHING ELSE, IT SHOULD GIVE P'GELL QUITE A SURPRISE!

I SAW THAT!

YOU'RE GONNA HAND IT OVER OR ELSE!

YOU'RE THE GUY WHO KILLED THAT JEWELER!

SO YOU KNOW I'M NOT KIDDIN' AROUND!

WELL, NEITHER AM I!

NEITHER AM I!

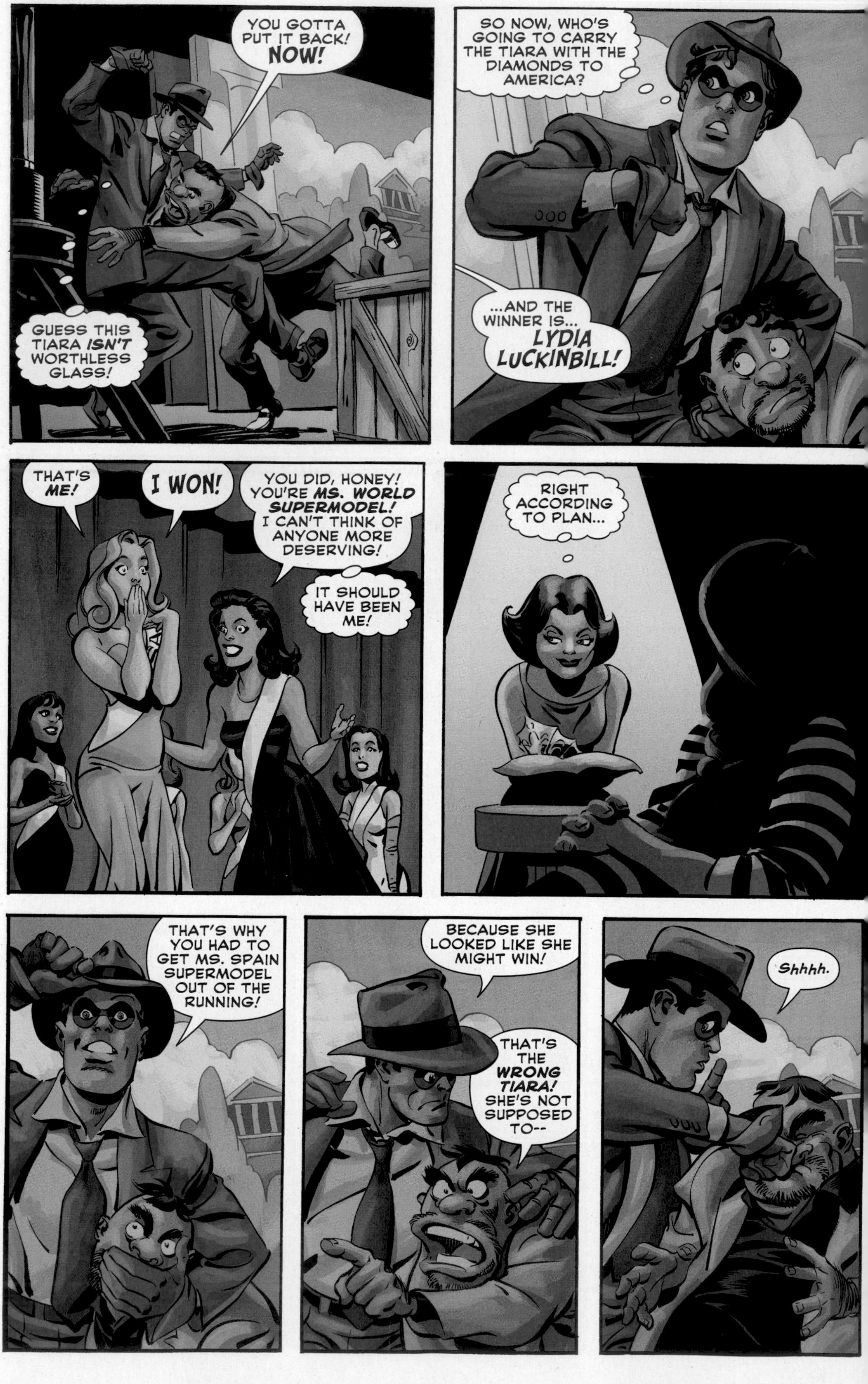
YOU GOTTA PUT IT BACK! NOW!
GUESS THIS TIARA ISN'T WORTHLESS GLASS!
SO NOW, WHO'S GOING TO CARRY THE TIARA WITH THE DIAMONDS TO AMERICA?
...AND THE WINNER IS... LYDIA LUCKINBILL!
THAT'S ME!
I WON!
YOU DID, HONEY! YOU'RE MS. WORLD SUPERMODEL! I CAN'T THINK OF ANYONE MORE DESERVING!
IT SHOULD HAVE BEEN ME!
RIGHT ACCORDING TO PLAN...
THAT'S WHY YOU HAD TO GET MS. SPAIN SUPERMODEL OUT OF THE RUNNING!
BECAUSE SHE LOOKED LIKE SHE MIGHT WIN!
THAT'S THE WRONG TIARA! SHE'S NOT SUPPOSED TO--
Shhhh.

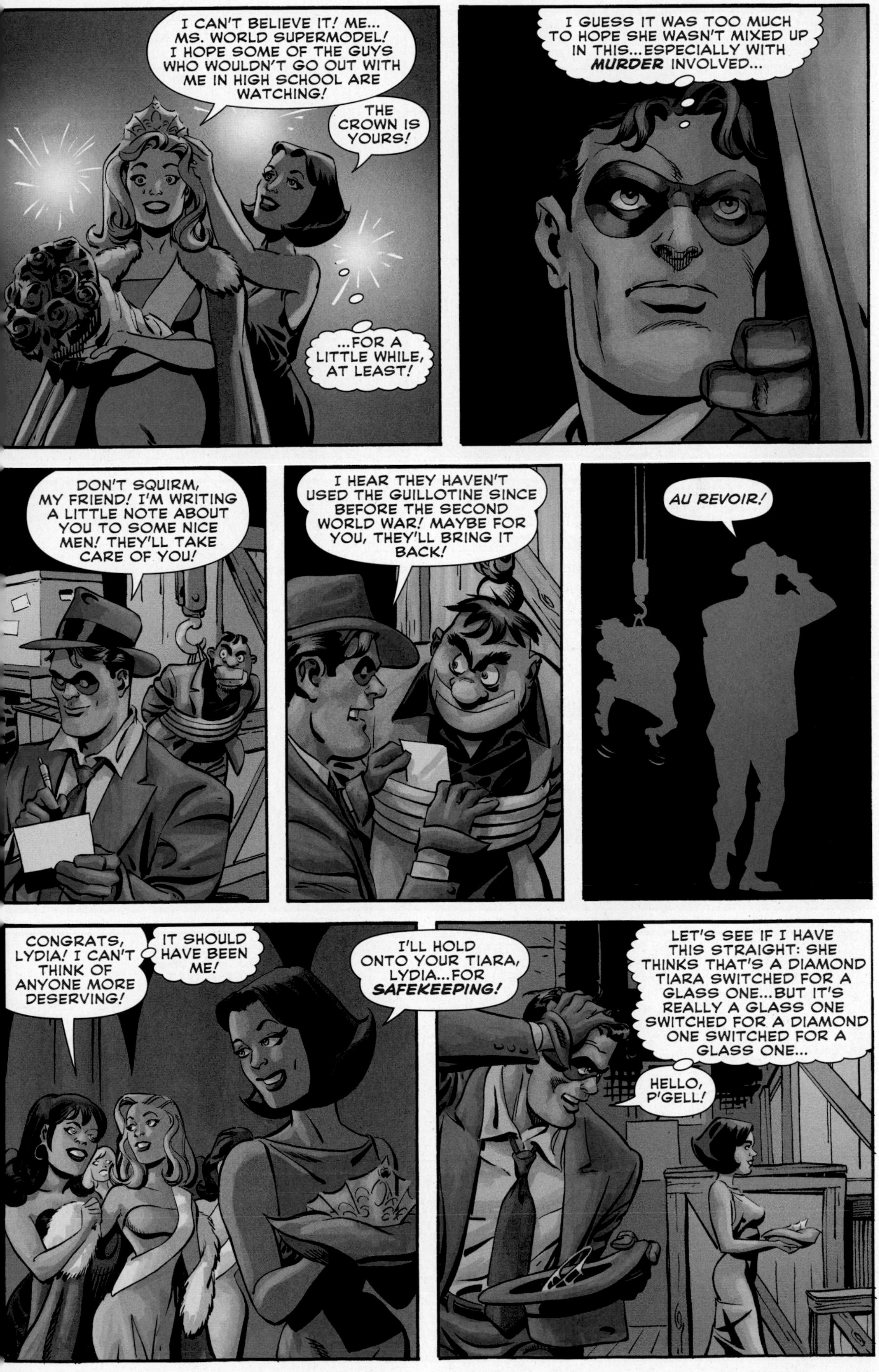
I CAN'T BELIEVE IT! ME... MS. WORLD SUPERMODEL! I HOPE SOME OF THE GUYS WHO WOULDN'T GO OUT WITH ME IN HIGH SCHOOL ARE WATCHING!
THE CROWN IS YOURS!
...FOR A LITTLE WHILE, AT LEAST!
I GUESS IT WAS TOO MUCH TO HOPE SHE WASN'T MIXED UP IN THIS...ESPECIALLY WITH MURDER INVOLVED...
DON'T SQUIRM, MY FRIEND! I'M WRITING A LITTLE NOTE ABOUT YOU TO SOME NICE MEN! THEY'LL TAKE CARE OF YOU!
I HEAR THEY HAVEN'T USED THE GUILLOTINE SINCE BEFORE THE SECOND WORLD WAR! MAYBE FOR YOU, THEY'LL BRING IT BACK!
AU REVOIR!
CONGRATS, LYDIA! I CAN'T THINK OF ANYONE MORE DESERVING!
IT SHOULD HAVE BEEN ME!
I'LL HOLD ONTO YOUR TIARA, LYDIA...FOR SAFEKEEPING!
LET'S SEE IF I HAVE THIS STRAIGHT: SHE THINKS THAT'S A DIAMOND TIARA SWITCHED FOR A GLASS ONE...BUT IT'S REALLY A GLASS ONE SWITCHED FOR A DIAMOND ONE SWITCHED FOR A GLASS ONE...
HELLO, P'GELL!

SPIRIT, MY DARLING! ARE YOU PERCHANCE GOING TO BE FLYING BACK WITH US TO THE STATES?

NO, I HAVE A LITTLE BUSINESS MATTER HERE TO TEND TO...

Another trip to la Maison de Diamond...

APRÈS VOUS, MADAME...

La M
de Dia

YES, I COULD GET TO LIKE THIS CITY QUITE A BIT...

And twelve hours later at Central City International Airport...

...the media and her friends gather to welcome the newly crowned Ms. World Supermodel...

CONGRATS, LYDIA!

AREN'T YOU EXCITED FOR LYDIA, DEAR?

IT SHOULD HAVE BEEN ME!

ISN'T IT A LITTLE PRETENTIOUS OF ME TO WEAR THE TIARA WHEN I GET OFF THE PLANE?

YOUR PUBLIC EXPECTS IT!

WHATEVER YOU SAY, P'GELL!

IN FACT, I THINK YOU SHOULD KEEP IT ON AT LEAST UNTIL WE PASS THROUGH CUSTOMS!

PEOPLE MAKE SUCH A FUSS OVER A LITTLE TIARA! I MEAN, IT'S ONLY MADE OF GLASS!

CUSTOMS

ANYTHING TO DECLARE?

JUST THAT I AM SO HAPPY TO BE BACK HOME IN AMERICA!

NO WONDER SHE WON.

WELL, I HAVE SOMETHING TO DECLARE! I DECLARE YOU THE MOST BEAUTIFUL WOMAN I'VE EVER SEEN!

AIRPORT SECURITY MAKES YOU FEEL SO SECURE.

I WANT TO THANK EVERYONE AND WISH FOR WORLD PEACE, MOTHERHOOD, THE LIBERATION OF ALL MINORITIES AND FREEDOM!

THAT ABOUT COVERS IT! SAY, MAYBE I SHOULD CARRY YOUR TIARA!

HERE IT IS, BUT WHAT'S THE BIG DEAL? IT'S JUST CHEAP GLASS!

HAVE YOU SEEN WHAT CHEAP GLASS TIARAS ARE GOING FOR ON eBAY THESE DAYS?

I'LL TAKE CARE OF IT!

BOY, WILL I TAKE CARE OF IT--!

HELLO.

THE TIARA, IF YOU DON'T MIND...

YOU'RE WELCOME TO TRY IT ON, COMMISSIONER, BUT I DON'T THINK IT GOES WITH YOUR COMPLEXION!

NICE TRY, P'GELL... BUT YOU PLAYING INNOCENT IS LIKE PARIS HILTON CRYING POVERTY.

EXAMINE IT, BAKER!

WE TRACKED DOWN THE PROSPECTIVE BUYERS AND FENCES, P'GELL! I FIGURED OUT YOUR ENTIRE PLAN...

...AND I DID IT WITH NO HELP WHATSOEVER FROM A CERTAIN GUY IN A BLUE SUIT!

ALL BY MYSELF!

SO WHAT DO YOU THINK IT'S WORTH, BAKER? TEN MILLION? TWENTY?

I'D SAY ABOUT SIX BUCKS ON eBAY.

WHAT!?

GLASS, COMMISSIONER. PURE, CHEAP GLASS!

BUT I HAD IT ALL FIGURED OUT... I DID...

TALK! WHAT HAVE YOU DONE WITH THE REAL DIAMONDS?

"REAL DIAMONDS"? WHY, WHATEVER DO YOU MEAN?

SEARCH HER! SEARCH EVERY SQUARE INCH OF HER!

ME, SIR?

NO, NOT YOU, HOTCHKISS! GET A FEMALE OFFICER!

But to no one's surprise, the search yields nothing...

YOU'RE SAYING THE DIAMONDS NEVER LEFT FRANCE?

NOPE. AND THE AUTHORITIES WILL RETURN THEM TO THEIR RIGHTFUL OWNER!

WE HAD TO LET P'GELL GO! ALL THE KILLERS ARE IN CUSTODY, HERE AND IN FRANCE! NONE OF THEM CAN IMPLICATE HER!

GIVE HER THE BENEFIT OF THE DOUBT, DOLAN! MAYBE SHE DIDN'T KNOW THE PLAN INVOLVED MURDER!

LINE TWO FOR YOU, COMMISSIONER! IT'S THE HEAD OF THE POLICE NATIONALE IN FRANCE!

THANKS, CARTER!

MAURICE! DON'T TELL ME...LET ME GUESS! YOU WANT TO THANK ME FOR THE BRILLIANT POLICE WORK THAT HELPED YOU RECOVER THOSE DIAMONDS!

NO, I'LL THANK HIM ON YOUR BEHALF! HE'S RIGHT HERE IN MY OFFICE.

I'M JUST TRYING TO DO MY JOB, COMMISSIONER!

JUST TRYING TO SOLVE A COUPLE MURDERS AND PREVENT OTHERS!

IN FACT, I SENSE ONE MORE IS ABOUT TO OCCUR!

AFTERNOON, LADIES!

EVERYTHING OKAY?

I CAN TELL BY YOUR CONVERSATION SOMETHING'S WRONG.

YOU **CAD!**

DO YOU KNOW WHAT YOU **DID?**

YEAH, I **KNOW** WHAT I **DID**...

I SAVED YOU FROM **GOING TO PRISON** FOR SMUGGLING... **THAT'S** WHAT I DID!

SHE'S REFERRING TO **THIS!**

I THOUGHT YOU WENT TO FRANCE TO WORK ON A **CASE!**

I **DID!**

P'GELL, EXPLAIN TO HER HOW ALL THE CONTESTANTS WERE JUST BEING GRATEFUL TO ME!

OH, SHE **EXPLAINED,** ALL RIGHT! SHE TOLD ME HOW YOU BEHAVED WITH THEM!

BUT I **DIDN'T**... THAT'S NOT TRUE...

YOU'RE SO MUCH BETTER OFF WITHOUT HIM, ELLEN!

I CAN'T IMAGINE WHAT KIND OF WOMAN WOULD WANT A MAN LIKE THAT!

YOU KNOW, SPIRIT...THERE ARE TIMES WHEN I THINK YOU'RE THE SMARTEST GUY I EVER MET. AND THEN...

DIAMOND SMUGGLERS AND MURDERERS ARE **EASY** TO FIGURE OUT, COMMISSIONER... IT'S THIS RELATIONSHIP STUFF THAT'S HARD...

THE END

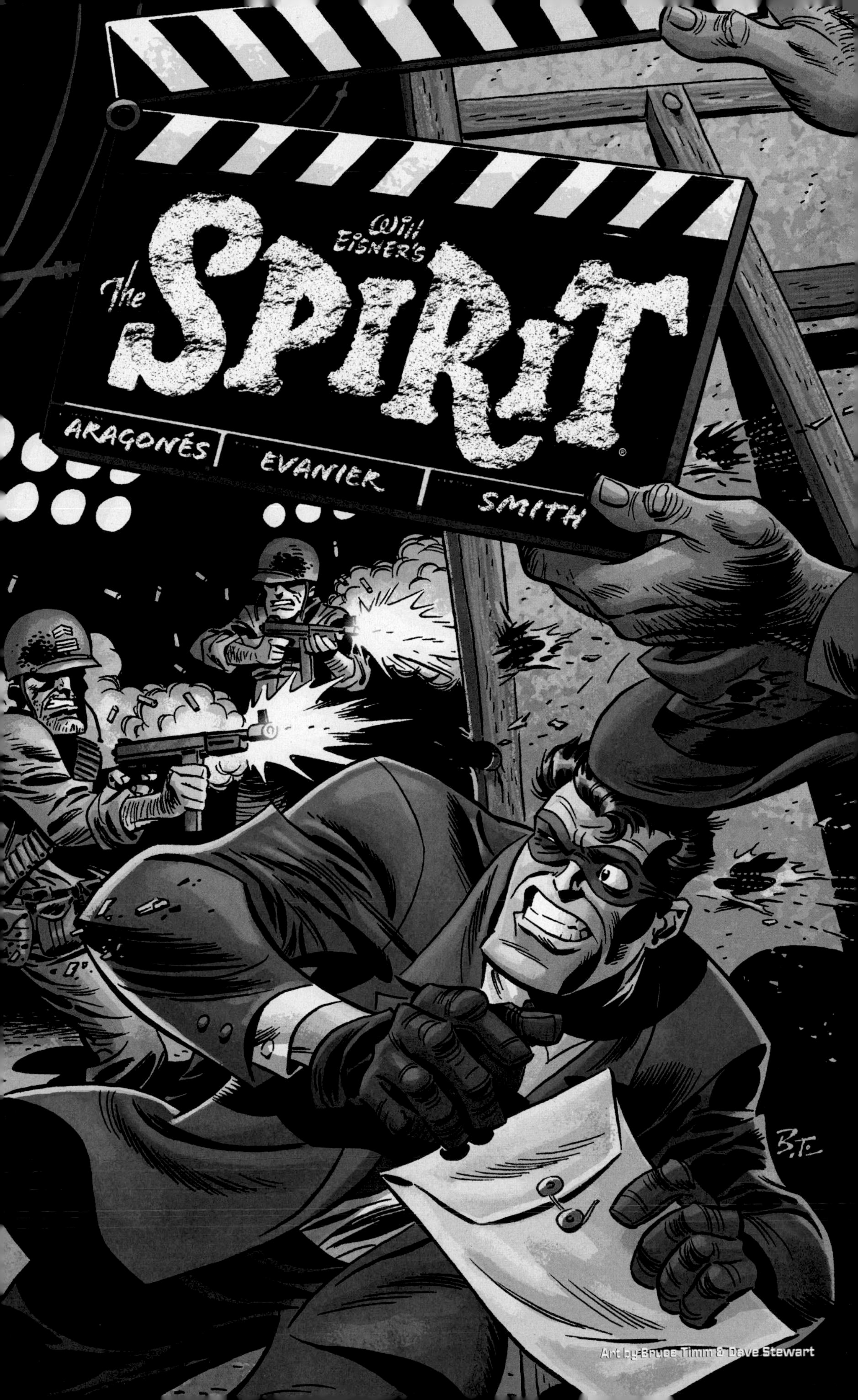
Will Eisner's
The SPIRIT
ARAGONÉS
EVANIER
SMITH
B.T.
Art by Bruce Timm & Dave Stewart

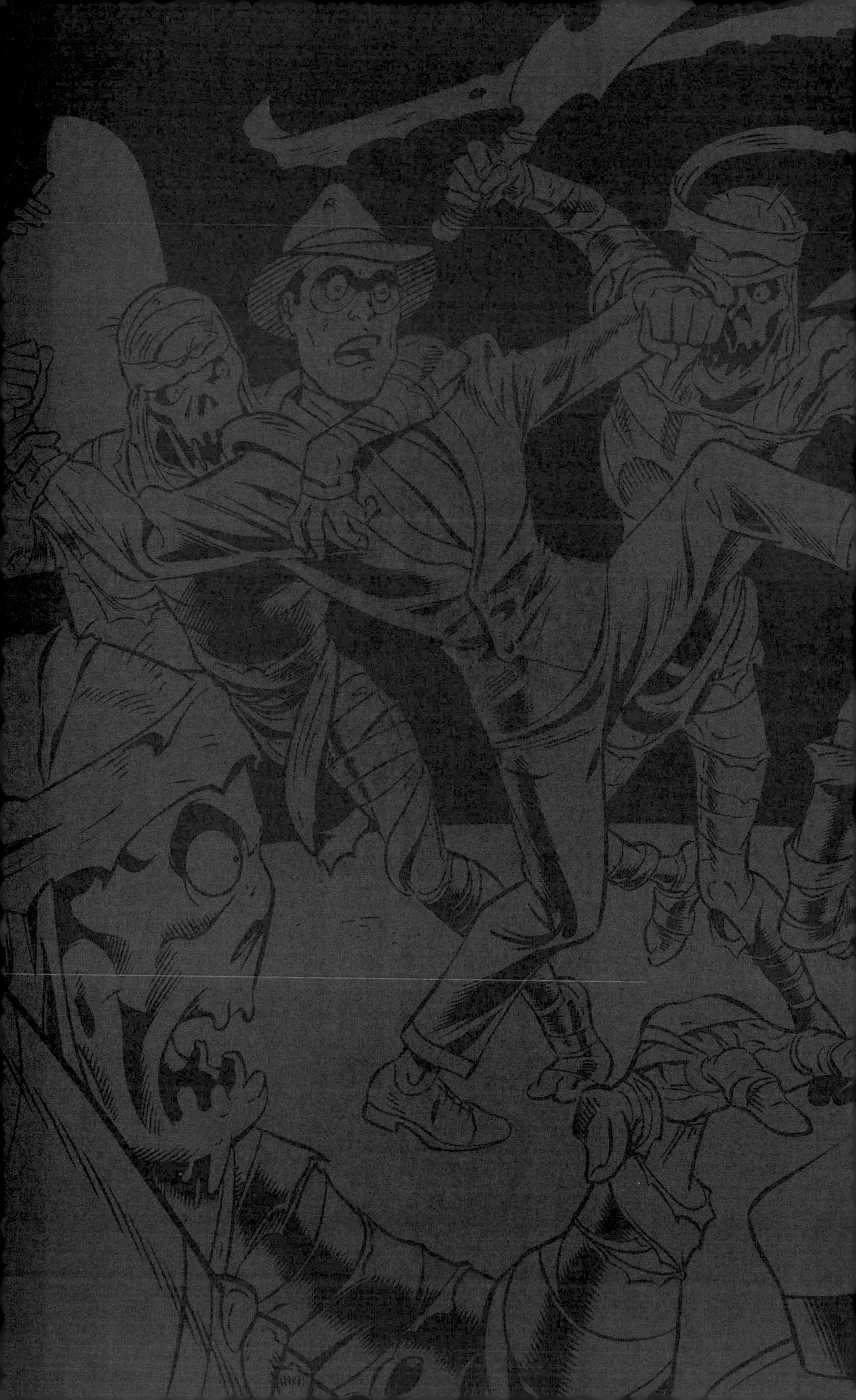

CAREFUL, MEN...THE ENEMY COULD BE ANY-WHERE...

...ANYWHERE AND *EVERYWHERE!*

BANG!

SARGE! GRUBER'S BEEN SHOT!

GET DOWN! ALL OF YOU! ESPECIALLY *YOU,* DAVIS!

DIDN'T YOU HEAR ME? I SAID *GET DOWN!*

I'M SCARED, SARGE! WE'RE *SITTIN' DUCKS* OUT HERE!

POW!

ARRR-GGGH!

HEY, *SARGE* ISN'T SUPPOSED TO DIE NOW!

STAND IN FOR MURDER

Written by
SERGIO ARAGONÉS
and **MARK EVANIER**

Illustrated by
PAUL SMITH

Lettered by
TODD KLEIN

Colored by
LEE LOUGHRIDGE

Assistant Editor
STEPHANIE BUSCEMA

Editor
JOEY CAVALIERI

The Spirit created by
WILL EISNER

Cover by **BRUCE TIMM**
Colored by **DAVE STEWART**

AND YOU, DEREK! THAT *"POW"* WASN'T FOR YOU! THAT WAS WILSON'S CUE! YOU'RE THE *STAR* OF THIS MOVIE, REMEMBER? SARGE DOESN'T DIE UNTIL SCENE 78-B...

...WHICH YOU'D *KNOW* IF YOU'D EVER BOTHERED TO READ THE SCRIPT! NOW, *GET UP* AND TRY IT AGAIN!

HE'S...HE'S DEAD!

NOT UNTIL SCENE 78-B...AND I HOPE HE'S A *LOT* MORE CONVINCING THEN THAN HE WAS JUST NOW!

DIDN'T YOU HEAR ME, DEREK? *GET UP!* FROM THE TOP!

CUT!

JEEZ! IF I'D WANTED BAD ACTING IN MY MOVIE, I WOULD HAVE HIRED SOMEBODY *BANKABLE!*

NO, I MEAN HE'S DEAD...AS IN, *FOR REAL!*

DEAD?! HOW COULD HE BE DEAD? I HAVE TWO-THIRDS OF A *PICTURE* TO SHOOT!

WELL, YOU'D BETTER FIND SOMEONE *ELSE* TO PLAY SGT. BLOCKER...BECAUSE DEREK SINCLAIR IS DEAD!

OH, WHAT THIS IS GOING TO DO TO MY SHOOTING SCHEDULE...

HAS AN AMBULANCE BEEN CALLED? OR THE POLICE?

MR. HELM, WE WERE WAITING FOR YOUR INSTRUCTIONS...

CALL THEM, FOR GOD'S SAKE! CALL THEM NOW!

CALL AN AMBULANCE OR THE POLICE!

CALL AN AMBULANCE OR THE POLICE!

AN AMBULANCE ARRIVES, FOLLOWED BY THE POLICE...

ALL RIGHT, NOBODY LEAVES THE SET...AND BY "NOBODY," I MEAN YOU, WHOEVER YOU MAY BE!

COMMISSIONER, IF THE EXTRAS STAY, THEY GO INTO OVER-TIME PAY! COULD WE AT LEAST RELEASE THEM?

NO.

WELL, SPIRIT... WHAT DO YOU THINK?

I THINK WE'D BETTER EXAMINE ALL THE GUNS AND FIGURE OUT WHICH ONE CONTAINED REAL AMMO INSTEAD OF BLANKS...

...THEN WE CAN START ASKING HOW IT GOT THERE!

I ALREADY PUT MY MEN ON THAT!

AFTER HOURS OF INTERROGATION, 'BOUT ALL THEY FIND OUT IS...

I LOADED ALL THE WEAPONS MYSELF...WITH *BLANKS!* OF THAT, I AM ABSOLUTELY CERTAIN!

SOMEONE SWAPPED OUT THE AMMO IN ONE WITH THE REAL STUFF!

THE REST OF THE GUNS WERE ALL STILL FULL OF BLANKS!

COMMISSIONER, THIS HAS ALREADY COST THE COMPANY A PARTIAL DAY OF FILMING...

AND IT'S ALREADY COST DEREK SINCLAIR THE REST OF HIS LIFE! WE'RE *INVESTIGATING!*

AND I'D BETTER NOT SEE ANY OF THIS AS A "SPECIAL FEATURE" ON THE *DVD!*

COMMISSIONER! THIS ACTOR IS HAL GUIDRY. HIS GUN FIRED THE FATAL SHOT!

I WAS ONLY FOLLOWING ORDERS!

THAT'S WHAT THEY ALL SAY WHEN THEY WEAR THAT UNIFORM.

NO, I MEAN I WAS HANDED THE WEAPON "HOT AND COCKED!" THAT MEANS "READY TO FIRE." I WAS TOLD TO FIRE IT ON CUE!

I DIDN'T *MEAN* TO KILL SINCLAIR...I DIDN'T EVEN *KNOW* HIM!

WHY DOES THIS *NOT* SMELL LIKE AN ACCIDENT?

I'VE BEEN NOT SMELLING THE SAME THING! I GAVE THEM THE OKAY TO MOVE THE BODY OUT...

ONE SIDE, PLEASE! *COMING THROUGH!*

NO! DON'T OPEN THOSE DOORS! YOU'LL LET *THEM* IN!

"*THEM*"?!

THE DREADED *PAPARAZZI!*

YOU'RE IN MY SHOT!

HEY, WE'RE TRYING TO GET HIM OUT OF HERE!

I'M NOT STOPPING YOU! AND BESIDES, HE'S ALREADY DEAD!

THIS IS THE COVER OF NEXT WEEK'S *ENQUIRER!* OR MAYBE *NEWS-WEEK!*

AND WHAT WAS YOUR RELATIONSHIP WITH SINCLAIR?

WE HAD A "SPECIAL BOND."

I THINK I'LL STICK AROUND FOR A WHILE.

I THINK I'LL GET AS FAR AS I CAN FROM THESE "SHOW BUSINESS" TYPES! I'M GOING BACK TO THE STATION. THE *C.S.I.* BOYS FOUND A *BROWN STAIN* NEAR WHERE THE GUNS WERE STORED, AND I WANT TO GET IT ANALYZED!

MAYBE I CAN GET SOME IDEA AS TO WHO WANTED SINCLAIR DEAD...

HOPE THIS DOESN'T CANCEL THE FILM!

YOU GOT ANY IDEA WHO KILLED HIM?

I DON'T WANT TO SAY ANYTHING WITH ALL THESE POLICE AROUND!

I MIGHT NOT TALK WITH ALL THESE POLICE AROUND EITHER!

SO...IS THE FILM ON OR OFF NOW? ARE WE OUTTA WORK?

NO, I'M GOING TO FINISH IT! THE STUDIO AND I OWE IT TO DEREK'S MEMORY. AND BESIDES, THINK OF THE CAMPAIGN-- "*SEE DEREK SINCLAIR'S FINAL PERFORMANCE!*"

WE DON'T EVEN NEED TO REPLACE HIM! WE CAN CONSTRUCT A *COMPUTER-GENERATED* DEREK SINCLAIR... DO IT ALL IN *C.G.I.!*

I GUESS NO ONE IS IRREPLACEABLE THESE DAYS...

GREAT! MAYBE YOU CAN DEDICATE THE FILM TO HIM!

IT'LL PROBABLY BE A BETTER FILM WITHOUT SINCLAIR!

SURE NO LOVE LOST BETWEEN THE TWO OF THEM! AND YOU KNOW WHY!

OF COURSE I KNOW WHY!

WELL, *I DON'T* KNOW WHY! AND QUESTIONING PEOPLE AND EAVESDROPPING DON'T SEEM TO BE TELLING ME WHY!

HEY! YOU WITH THE MASK! YOU'RE ON THE WRONG SET!

I AM?

OF COURSE! *"EL COYOTE NEGRO"* IS SHOOTING OVER ON *SIX!*

YOU PROBABLY MISSED YOUR CALL TIME BY NOW!

DON'T WORRY...THEY'RE NOT FILMING YET. EVERYONE'S STANDING AROUND TALKING ABOUT DEREK SINCLAIR!

HEY, THAT MIGHT BE INTERESTING TO LISTEN IN ON...

AH, I SEE YOU ALREADY HAVE YOUR MASK, AND IT'S JUST FABULOUS! BUT THE REST OF THE OUTFIT IS WRONG, ALL WRONG!

JUST LIKE THAT?

TAKE IT OFF!

COME ON, COME ON! THEY'RE WAITING FOR YOU ON THE SET!

HEY, WHO DO *YOU* THINK WANTED DEREK SINCLAIR KILLED?

APART FROM EVERYONE WITH AN OUNCE OF TASTE? ONLY HALF THE MEN IN THIS AREA CODE!

ALL THOSE SCARS YOU HAVE...YOU MUST DO A LOT OF YOUR OWN STUNTS!

IN MY PARTICULAR LINE OF WORK, I HAVE TO!

ANYONE IN *PARTICULAR* WHO MIGHT HAVE KILLED HIM? ANYONE WHO WAS WORKING IN THAT WAR MOVIE?

WELL, YOU KNOW ABOUT HIM AND THE PRODUCER'S WIFE...

NO, I *DON'T* KNOW ABOUT HIM AND THE PRODUCER'S WIFE!

WORST-KEPT SECRET SINCE SINATRA'S HAIRPIECE!

AH, YOU REALLY LOOK THE PART! *EL COYOTE NEGRO!* THE GREATEST OF ALL SWASHBUCKLERS!

JUST GIVE ME A SWASH AND I'LL BUCKLE IT!

I WAS RIGHT. YOU LEARN MORE FROM HOLLYWOOD TYPES WHEN THEY'RE GOSSIPING RATHER THAN TALKING TO *"THE LAW!"*

ON TO MAKE-UP! THEY'RE WAITING!

SAY, I HEAR THE PRODUCER'S WIFE WANTED SINCLAIR DEAD!

NOT AS MUCH AS HIS LEADING LADY, NANCY ASTOR! HE DUMPED HER FOR SOME HOT BABE OF A STARLET!

MAY I REMOVE YOUR MASK?

NO.

I GUESS YOU DON'T NEED MAKE-UP **UNDER** THE MASK! HEY, WHO DO **YOU** THINK KILLED DEREK SINCLAIR?

I THINK EITHER THE PRODUCER'S WIFE OR NANCY ASTOR. WHO DO **YOU** THINK DUNNIT?

I THINK IT'S OBVIOUS... **BRUCE RICO!** HE WANTED THAT PART **SO** BADLY! SAID IT WAS HIS "OSCAR ROLE." HIS BREAKTHROUGH PART!

OKAY, I THINK YOU'RE DONE, SPORT!

HEY, I LOOK DARN GOOD WITH A MUSTACHE!

RICO THOUGHT HE HAD A LOCK ON THE ROLE OF SARGE. THAT WAS BEFORE SINCLAIR AND THE PRODUCER'S WIFE!

HEY, YOU KNOW, YOU LOOK DARN GOOD WITH A MUSTACHE!

I HEARD HELM DIDN'T WANT SINCLAIR FOR THAT WAR PIC! THE PRODUCER INSISTED... OR RATHER, HIS WIFE DID!

SO NOW I KNOW WHO WANTED SINCLAIR DEAD: **JUST ABOUT EVERY-BODY!** WONDER IF ANYONE WANTED HIM ALIVE...

...**BESIDES** THE PRODUCER'S WIFE!

MEANWHILE, BACK IN WARDROBE...

WHAT DO YOU MEAN YOU DON'T **HAVE** MY COYOTE NEGRO COSTUME?

WHAT I SAID! YOU'VE BEEN REPLACED!

THEY GAVE THE JOB TO A NEW GUY...MUCH BETTER LOOKING, **PLUS** HE HAD HIS OWN MASK!

THE UNION'S GONNA HEAR ABOUT THIS!

SINCE WHEN IS BEING **HANDSOME** A REQUIREMENT TO WORK IN MOVIES?

ON THE SET...

THERE SEEMS TO BE ANOTHER *EL COYOTE NEGRO* ON THE PREMISES!

QUIET *ON THE SET!* WE NEED *QUIET!*

READY...AND *ACTION!*

...AND *CUT!* THAT'S A PRINT! *GREAT!*

I'LL BE IN MY TRAILER WHEN YOU NEED ME!

YOU'RE ON!

THAT'S RIGHT, *YOU!* GET OUT THERE--AND HURRY!

KISSING BEAUTIFUL ACTRESSES IS A *MUCH* BETTER JOB THAN POLICE WORK! NO ONE TRYING TO BEAT ME UP...

READY...AND *ACTION!*

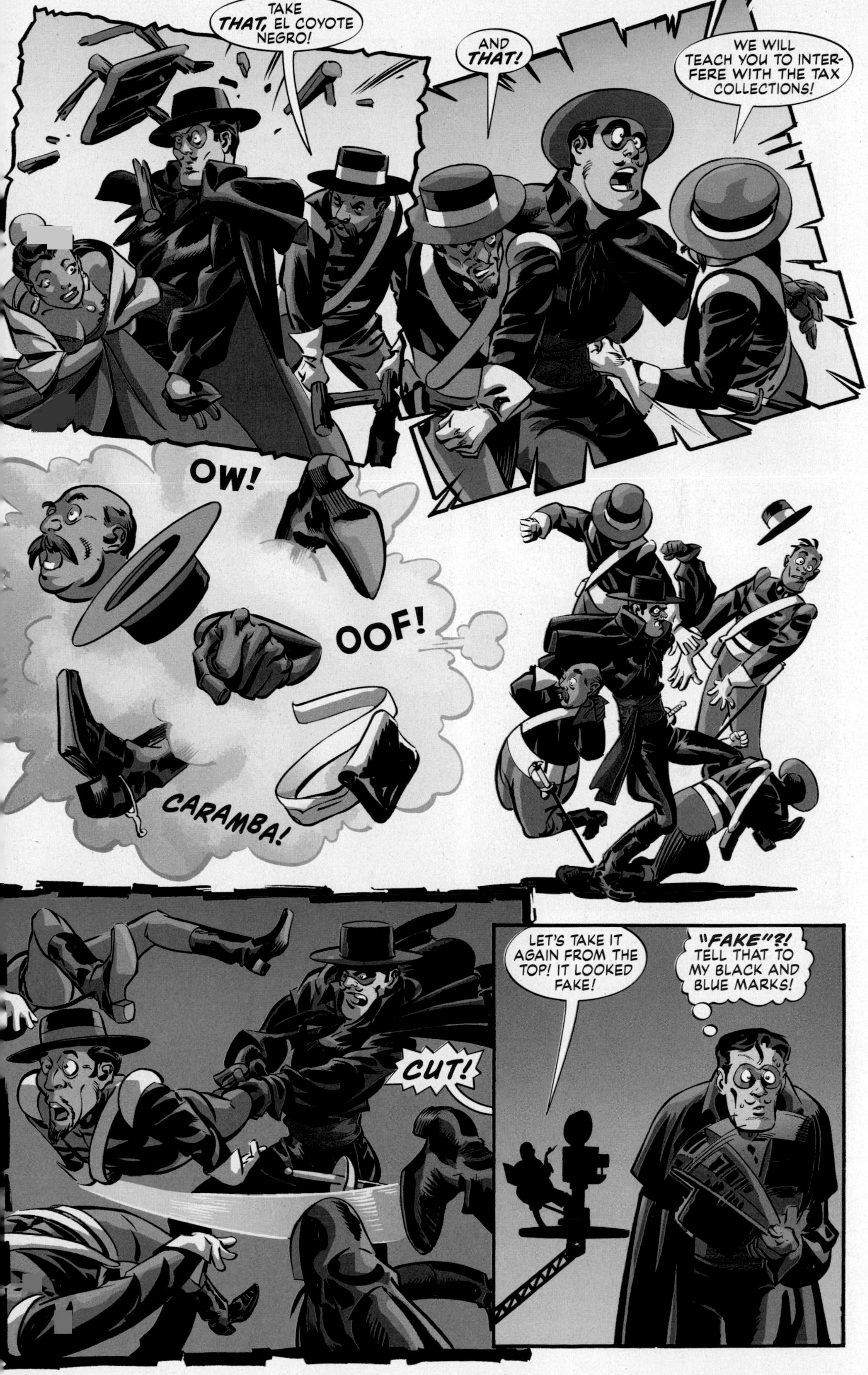
TAKE THAT, EL COYOTE NEGRO!
AND THAT!
WE WILL TEACH YOU TO INTERFERE WITH THE TAX COLLECTIONS!
OW!
OOF!
CARAMBA!
CUT!
LET'S TAKE IT AGAIN FROM THE TOP! IT LOOKED FAKE!
"FAKE"?! TELL THAT TO MY BLACK AND BLUE MARKS!

SIX TAKES LATER...

WHERE'D YOU LEARN TO PULL YOUR PUNCHES, FELLA? YOU WERE ACTUALLY HITTING US!

I WAS? SORRY.

BUT YOU MADE ME LOOK *MUY MACHO!*

SINCLAIR HAD DOUBLE-CROSSED THIS FINANCIER NAMED LORENZO!

PHIL SAID IT WAS COLOMBIAN DRUG LORDS!

MORE SUSPECTS...

COLOMBIAN DRUG LORDS, BUT FROM NORWAY!

SINCLAIR TOLD ME HE WAS INVOLVED WITH A WEALTHY, POWERFUL WOMAN AND THAT IF HER HUSBAND FOUND OUT, HE'D BE DEAD!

AND *MORE* SUSPECTS...

OH, *I* KNOW WHO IT IS! I SAW THEM TOGETHER ONCE IN A RESTAURANT, NECKING IN A BACK BOOTH...

...IT WAS THE WIFE OF THE *MAYOR!*

I'D BETTER START CALLING IN SOME OF THESE SUSPECTS TO DOLAN.

MAYBE ONE OF THEM WILL CONNECT WITH THAT STAIN THEY FOUND...

...BUT THAT'LL HAVE TO WAIT! I'M NEEDED ON THE SET!

PLACES!

LET'S SEE...IT MIGHT BE THE PRODUCER, THE PRODUCER'S WIFE, THE LEADING LADY, SOMEBODY NAMED BRUCE RICO, THE DIRECTOR, A FINANCIER NAMED LORENZO, THE MAYOR'S WIFE...

...OH--CAN'T FORGET THOSE NORWEGIAN COLOMBIAN DRUG LORDS...

GOOD NIGHT, MY DEAR COYOTE...

...AND *CUT!* OKAY, BRING IN THE DOUBLE!

NEXT SHIFT!

THANKS FOR DOING THE HARD PART FOR ME.

HAVE TO REMEMBER NOT TO ACTUALLY HIT THE OTHER PEOPLE...

...AND *ACTION!*

WATCH OUT, COYOTE!

UH-OH.

"UH-OH" IS RIGHT!

WE SHALL DRAG HIM THROUGH THE STREETS OF SANTA DOMINGO!

THAT WILL TEACH THE RABBLE TO CROSS SEÑOR DOMENECH!

FIVE TAKES LATER...

*IRVING BERLIN WAS WRONG. EVERYTHING ABOUT IT **ISN'T** APPEALING...*

NICE JOB, PAL! YOU'LL BE GOOD FOR THE CANYON PLUNGE TOMORROW!

*THIS IS **ACTING?** I THINK DEREK SINCLAIR GOT OFF LUCKY!*

YOU'RE DONE FOR THE DAY, HON! 5:30 AM CALL TOMORROW MORNING!

I'D BETTER SOLVE THIS ONE IN A HURRY. LET'S SEE IF THE CRIME SCENE BOYS ARE OF ANY HELP...

AT THE POLICE STATION...

SPIRIT ON LINE ONE, SIR!

PROBABLY LUXURIATING ON SOME MOVIE SET WHILE THE REST OF US ARE WORKING!

THE COMPUTER'S STILL TRYING TO IDENTIFY THAT STAIN! IT'S NOT A DOUBLE MOCHA SKIM LATTE LIKE I THOUGHT...

I HAVE **SUSPECTS** FOR YOU, DOLAN: THE PRODUCER OF THE MOVIE, HIS WIFE, THE DIRECTOR, NANCY ASTOR THE LEADING LADY, AN ACTOR NAMED BRUCE RICO, SOME FINANCIER NAMED LORENZO...

THOSE ARE SOME PRETTY IMPORTANT SUSPECTS TO BE INVESTIGATING...

WAIT! YOU HAVEN'T HEARD THE BEST ONE! *THE MAYOR'S WIFE!*

THE MAYOR'S WIFE?! YOU MEAN THE MAYOR WHO KEEPS WANTING TO SLASH THE BUDGET, RETIRE ME AND BRING A YOUNGER MAN IN TO RUN THINGS?

THAT MAYOR'S WIFE?

I'M GOING TO HAVE **SO MANY** PEOPLE MAD AT ME.

TELL THE SPIRIT WE'RE CLOSE TO IDENTIFYING THAT STAIN!

YOU'D BETTER BE RIGHT ABOUT ONE OF THESE, SPIRIT! OR ELSE!

ONE CAN ONLY HOPE.

SHORTLY...

NOW, WHEN YOU INTERROGATE THESE SUSPECTS, BE **POLITE** AND ABOVE ALL, BE **DISCREET**! WE DON'T WANT TO OFFEND IMPORTANT PEOPLE...

...AND WE **REALLY** DON'T WANT IT GETTING OUT SO WE WIND UP WITH A **MEDIA CIRCUS**!

YOU CAN COUNT ON US, SIR.

WE'LL MAKE **SURE** THE PRESS DOESN'T GET WIND OF IT.

I WONDER IF STAND-INS ARE ALLOWED TO HAVE STAND-INS?

CAN'T WAIT TO GET OUT OF THIS SILLY CRIMEFIGHTER'S OUTFIT AND INTO MY OWN!

ROUGH DAY ON YOUR SET, MURRAY?

BRUTAL. YOU MUST BE HAPPY NOT TO HAVE THAT JERK SINCLAIR AROUND!

HEY, I OWE MY LIFE TO THAT JERK! IF HE HADN'T SHOVED ME ASIDE, THAT BULLET WOULD HAVE HIT ME!

FIRST TIME HE WAS EVER ON CUE IN HIS LIFE!

SAY THAT AGAIN!

WHAT YOU JUST SAID! SAY IT AGAIN!

OH. WELL, IN THE SCENE, I PLAY THIS SCARED GREEN RECRUIT...WE'RE CHARGING INTO BATTLE WITH THE ENEMY ALL AROUND US...

I WAS SUPPOSED TO GET SHOT, BUT THE SARGE--I MEAN SINCLAIR-- HE WAS CONFUSED! HE THOUGHT WE WERE IN ANOTHER SCENE...

...HE HADN'T REALLY STUDIED HIS SCRIPT--SAID HE WAS OUT LAST NIGHT WITH SOME GUY'S WIFE...

HE WAS SUPPOSED TO SHOVE ME ASIDE IN SCENE 78-B! WE WERE SHOOTING 22-C!

LUCKY FOR YOU!

...AND *UN*LUCKY FOR SINCLAIR.

SO HAVE I BEEN LOOKING IN THE WRONG DIRECTION?

PETE...THAT'S YOUR NAME, ISN'T IT? PETE? IS THERE ANYBODY IN THE WORLD--*ANYBODY*--WHO'D HAVE A REASON TO WANT YOU DEAD?

ME? NO...I'M JUST A NOBODY! NEVER HURT ANYONE...NEVER EVEN GOT NOTICED MUCH...

THAT'S WHY I BECAME AN ACTOR! THOUGHT IT MIGHT MAKE SOMEONE NOTICE I WAS ALIVE! SO FAR, IT HASN'T WORKED!

THINK HARD! ANYBODY AT ALL? A JEALOUS BOYFRIEND? A LOVER?

I DON'T HAVE A LOVER SO THERE ARE NO JEALOUS BOYFRIENDS! NO, I'M JUST AN AVERAGE GUY...NOT EVEN MAKING A LIVING...

DO YOU HAVE A CELL PHONE? I NEED TO CALL THE STATION.

HERE YOU GO... BUT I'M TELLING YOU. NOBODY HAD A REASON TO WANT ME KILLED!

WHERE ARE YOU TAKING ME?

AWAY FROM WHERE ANYONE TRYING TO KILL YOU WOULD EXPECT YOU TO BE!

DOLAN? ANY WORD ON THAT *BROWN STAIN* YET?

"CHEWING TOBACCO"?!

PETE...DO YOU KNOW ANY-ONE WHO CHEWS TOBACCO?

YEAH, MY BOOKIE...HAL GUIDRY! HEY, I GOTTA CALL THAT GUY! I PUT A HUGE BET DOWN TODAY ON THE FIFTH RACE AT BELMONT LAST NIGHT! DIDN'T HEAR WHO WON!

I HAVE A HUNCH I KNOW!

HEY, MILT! YOU HAPPEN TO HEAR WHAT HORSE WON THE FIFTH RACE AT BELMONT LAST NIGHT?

SURE! THE LONG SHOT, *BUENA FORTUNA!* CAME IN AT FORTY-TO-ONE!

THAT'S THE ONE I BET!

YAHOO! I'M RICH! I HAD A TIP AND I BET THE FARM ON THAT NAG!

GET DOWN!

KRASSHH!

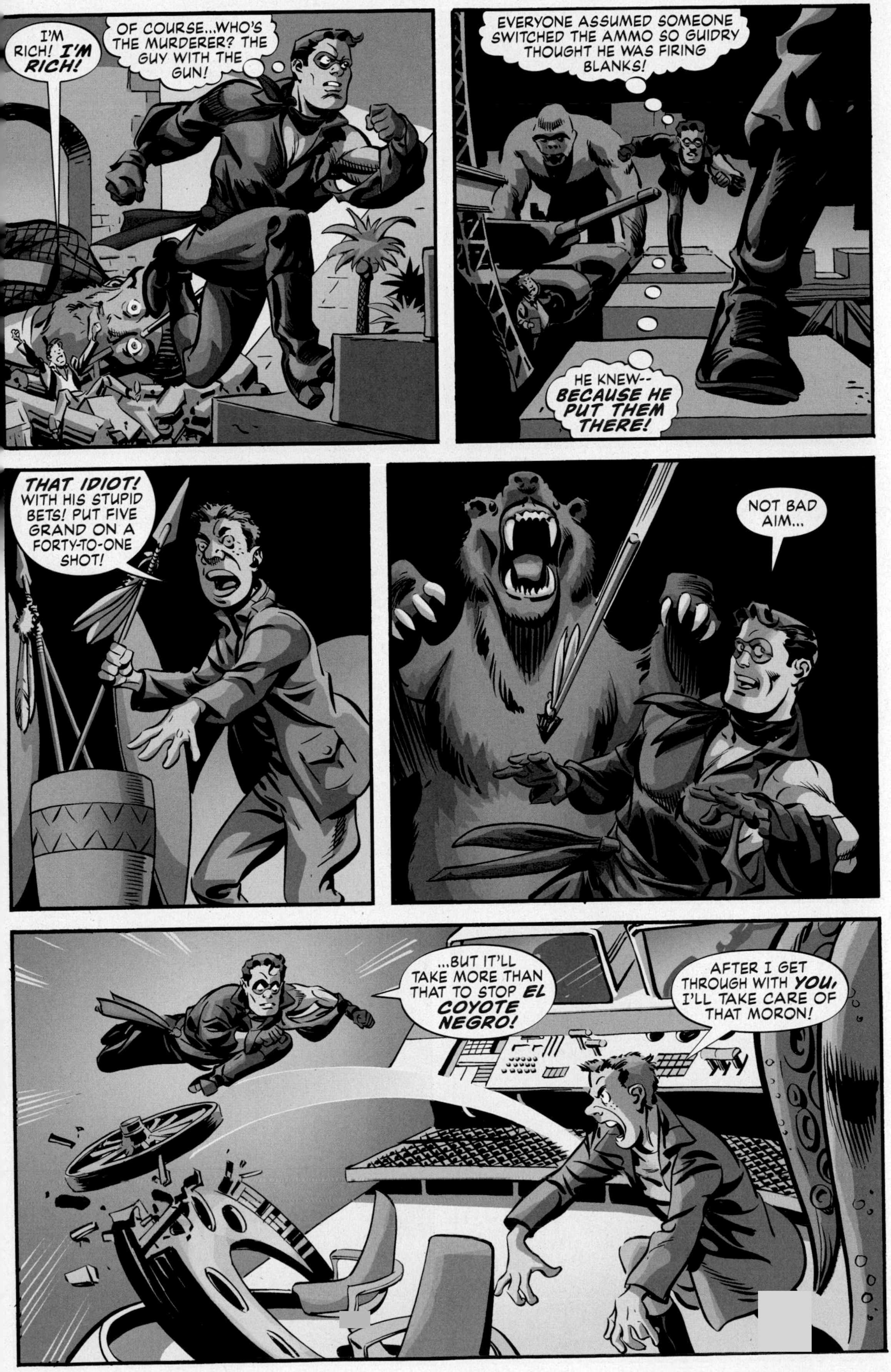

I'M RICH! I'M RICH!
OF COURSE...WHO'S THE MURDERER? THE GUY WITH THE GUN!
EVERYONE ASSUMED SOMEONE SWITCHED THE AMMO SO GUIDRY THOUGHT HE WAS FIRING BLANKS!
HE KNEW-- BECAUSE HE PUT THEM THERE!
THAT IDIOT! WITH HIS STUPID BETS! PUT FIVE GRAND ON A FORTY-TO-ONE SHOT!
NOT BAD AIM...
...BUT IT'LL TAKE MORE THAN THAT TO STOP EL COYOTE NEGRO!
AFTER I GET THROUGH WITH YOU, I'LL TAKE CARE OF THAT MORON!

AND I'M CERTAINLY NOT LETTING SOME SECOND-RATE *STAND-IN* GET IN MY WAY!

LET ME GUESS: YOU NEVER EVEN PLACED PETE'S BET... JUST KEPT THE FIVE GRAND...

WHY SHOULD I PLACE A STUPID BET HE HAD NO CHANCE OF WINNING?

JUST LIKE YOU GOT NO CHANCE OF WINNING *THIS*, FELLA!

HEY, YOU KNOW YOUR SWORDS...

OF COURSE! YOU KNOW THAT DUELING SCENE IN TOM CRUISE'S LAST FILM? WHO DO YOU THINK *STUNT-DOUBLED* HIM?

KNOCKED THE SWORD FROM THE OTHER GUY'S HAND *JUST LIKE THIS!*

NOW, *YOU DIE!*

I WOULD THINK A MASTER SWORDSMAN WOULD KNOW A PROP SWORD WHEN HE SAW ONE.

HA! WHEN DO I GET MY MONEY?

I'M AFRAID YOU MAY HAVE TO WAIT A WHILE, PETE. I'D SAY TWENTY YEARS TO LIFE...

AND SO...

EXCUSE ME! THAT *MASK* IS STUDIO PROPERTY, I BELIEVE?

YOU KNOW, I HELPED HIM GET THE PART ON THIS FILM!

WHO SAYS THERE'S NO LOYALTY IN THE MOVIE BUSINESS?

I GUESS ALL THAT'S LEFT OF THIS CASE IS TO TAKE OUR FRIEND TO THE STATION...

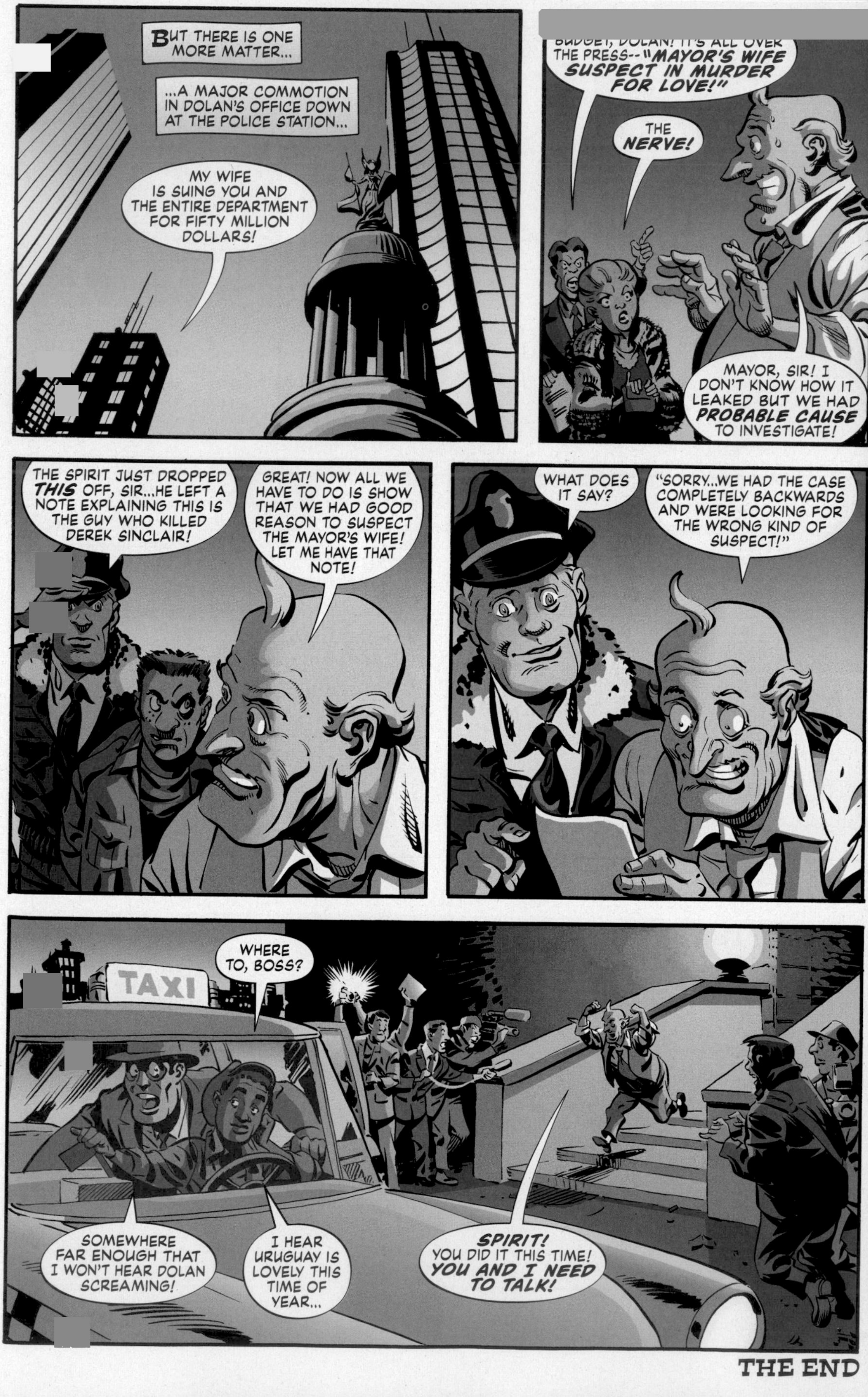
BUT THERE IS ONE MORE MATTER...
...A MAJOR COMMOTION IN DOLAN'S OFFICE DOWN AT THE POLICE STATION...
MY WIFE IS SUING YOU AND THE ENTIRE DEPARTMENT FOR FIFTY MILLION DOLLARS!
BUDGET, DOLAN! IT'S ALL OVER THE PRESS-- "MAYOR'S WIFE SUSPECT IN MURDER FOR LOVE!"
THE NERVE!
MAYOR, SIR! I DON'T KNOW HOW IT LEAKED BUT WE HAD PROBABLE CAUSE TO INVESTIGATE!
THE SPIRIT JUST DROPPED THIS OFF, SIR...HE LEFT A NOTE EXPLAINING THIS IS THE GUY WHO KILLED DEREK SINCLAIR!
GREAT! NOW ALL WE HAVE TO DO IS SHOW THAT WE HAD GOOD REASON TO SUSPECT THE MAYOR'S WIFE! LET ME HAVE THAT NOTE!
WHAT DOES IT SAY?
"SORRY...WE HAD THE CASE COMPLETELY BACKWARDS AND WERE LOOKING FOR THE WRONG KIND OF SUSPECT!"
TAXI
WHERE TO, BOSS?
SOMEWHERE FAR ENOUGH THAT I WON'T HEAR DOLAN SCREAMING!
I HEAR URUGUAY IS LOVELY THIS TIME OF YEAR...
SPIRIT! YOU DID IT THIS TIME! YOU AND I NEED TO TALK!

THE END

Art by Paul Smith & Lee Loughridge

So one day, Ellen Dolan decides she needs a vacation...

I NEED A VACATION.

CINDY, LORI AND I HAVE BOOKED A CRUISE ON THE *CARIBBEAN QUEST!*

IT'S A GREAT ITINERARY-- *TWENTY-THREE* CITIES IN *ELEVEN* DAYS! IT'S FOR PEOPLE WHO JUST WANT TO BE ABLE TO SAY THEY'VE BEEN PLACES, NEVER MIND THAT THEY DIDN'T *SEE* ANYTHING!

SOUNDS THRILLING! I, uh, DON'T SUPPOSE THERE WILL BE ANY ELIGIBLE *MEN* ABOARD?

IF THERE *AREN'T,* WE'RE GOING TO JUMP SHIP AND *SWIM BACK!* AND NOT JUST *"ANY"* MEN! WE'RE EXPECTING TO MEET THE SOPHISTICATED, CHARMING KIND! MEN WHO KNOW HOW TO TREAT A LADY!

I THOUGHT THEY STOPPED MAKING THOSE ABOUT THE SAME TIME AS THE BETAMAX!

THEY'LL BE SUCH A WELCOME CHANGE FROM SOME OF THE MEN IN *THIS* CITY!

THERE ARE TIMES WHEN ELLEN'S ABOUT AS SUBTLE AS THE FINALE OF A GALLAGHER CONCERT!

SOME OF US, HOWEVER, HAVE *WORK* TO DO!

SO LONG! IF WE HAVE AN EXTRA FORTY SECONDS IN PUERTO VALLARTA, I'LL SEND YOU A POSTCARD!

THINKING OF TAGGING ALONG WITH THEM, SPIRIT?

NO CHANCE. ELEVEN DAYS ON A SHIP AND I'D BE SO BORED, I'D START PRAYING TO RAM AN ICEBERG, JUST TO MAKE THINGS INTERESTING!

BESIDES, YOU WANTED ME TO CHECK OUT THAT *ARGOSY* INSURANCE CALL, REMEMBER?

But Ellen isn't the only one shoving off to sea...

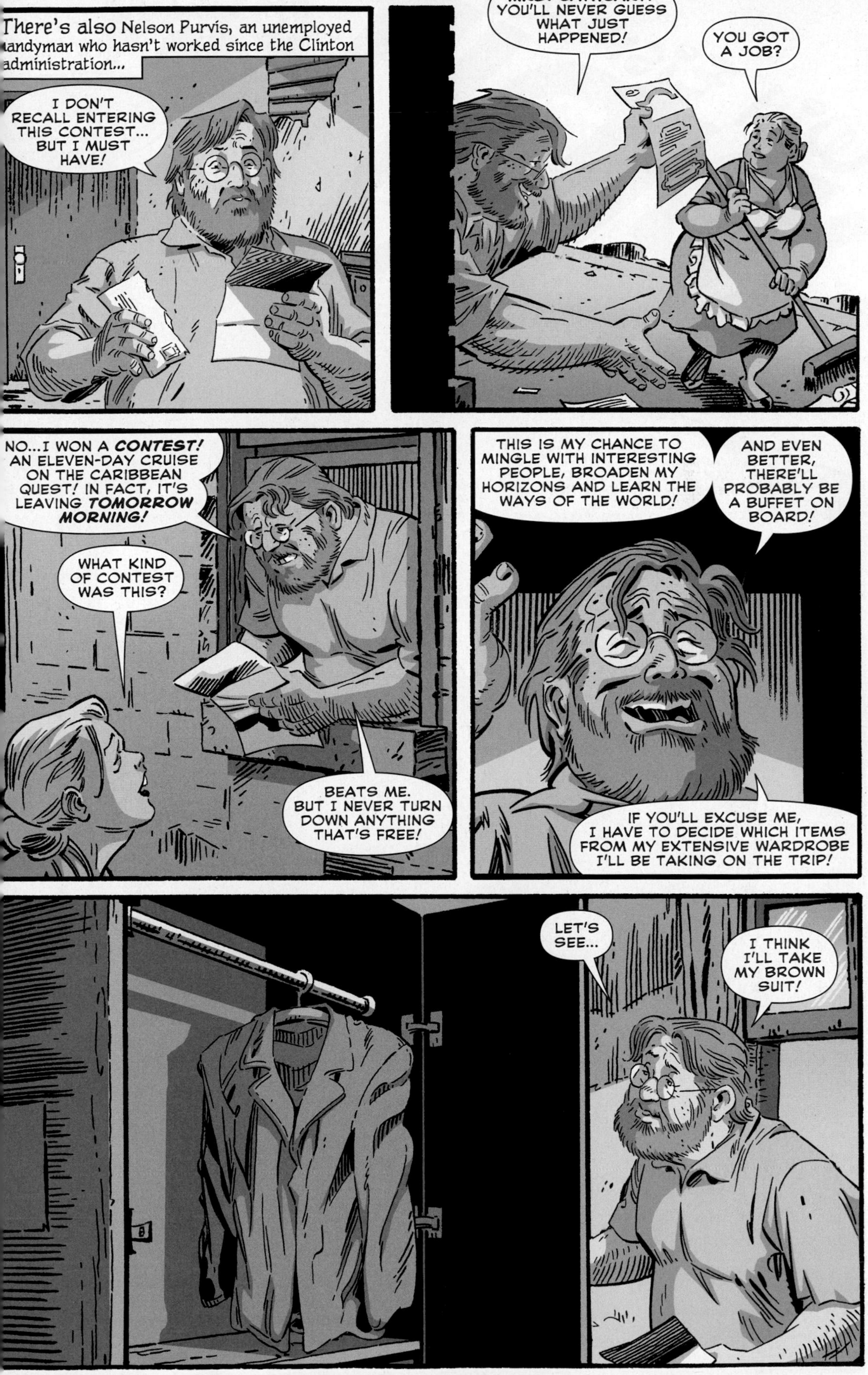
There's also Nelson Purvis, an unemployed handyman who hasn't worked since the Clinton administration...
I DON'T RECALL ENTERING THIS CONTEST... BUT I MUST HAVE!
MRS. CATHCART! YOU'LL NEVER GUESS WHAT JUST HAPPENED!
YOU GOT A JOB?
NO...I WON A CONTEST! AN ELEVEN-DAY CRUISE ON THE CARIBBEAN QUEST! IN FACT, IT'S LEAVING TOMORROW MORNING!
WHAT KIND OF CONTEST WAS THIS?
BEATS ME. BUT I NEVER TURN DOWN ANYTHING THAT'S FREE!
THIS IS MY CHANCE TO MINGLE WITH INTERESTING PEOPLE, BROADEN MY HORIZONS AND LEARN THE WAYS OF THE WORLD!
AND EVEN BETTER, THERE'LL PROBABLY BE A BUFFET ON BOARD!
IF YOU'LL EXCUSE ME, I HAVE TO DECIDE WHICH ITEMS FROM MY EXTENSIVE WARDROBE I'LL BE TAKING ON THE TRIP!
LET'S SEE...
I THINK I'LL TAKE MY BROWN SUIT!

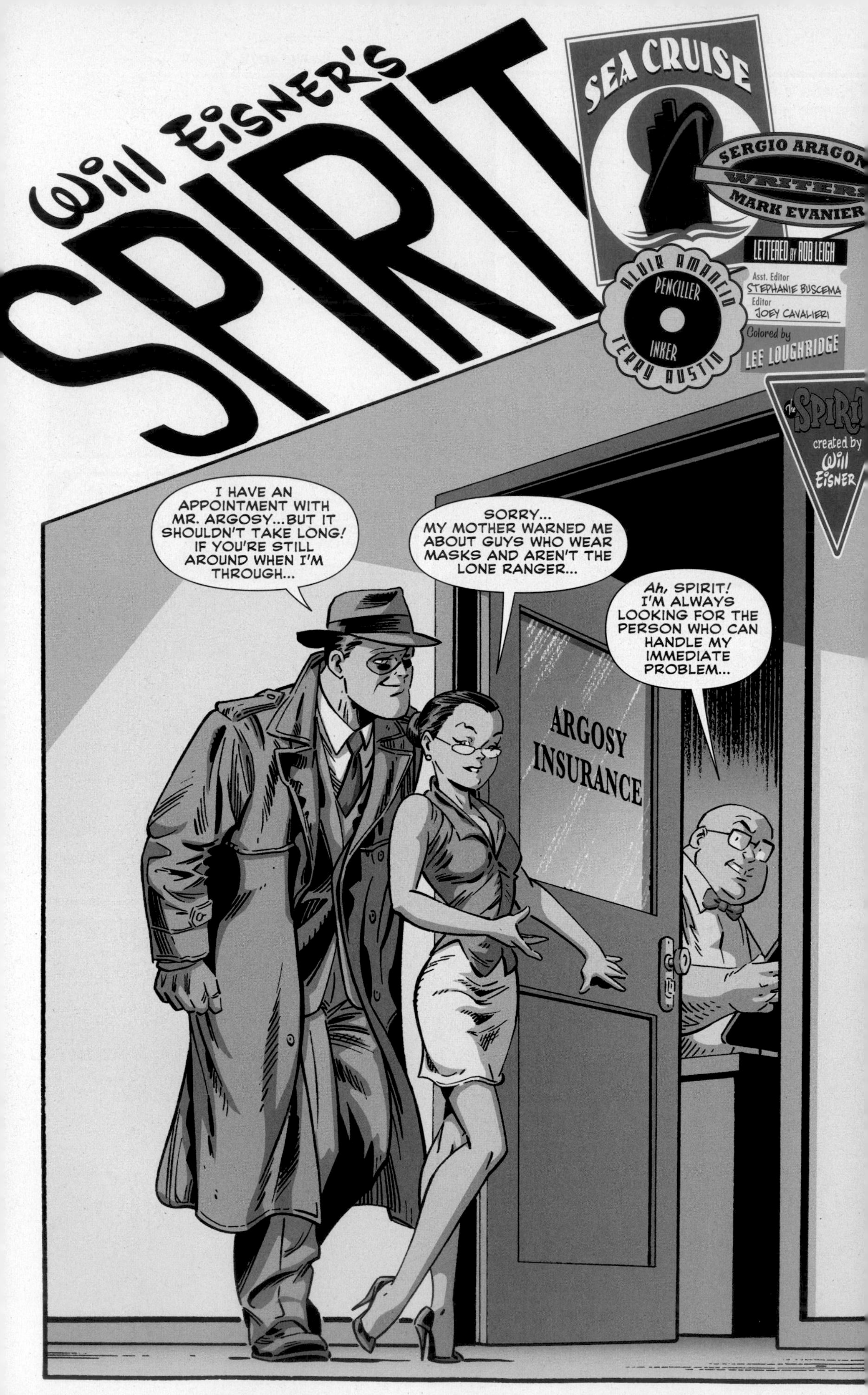

Will Eisner's
SPIRIT
SEA CRUISE
SERGIO ARAGONÉS
WRITERS
MARK EVANIER
LETTERED BY ROB LEIGH
ALDIR AMANCIO
PENCILLER
INKER
TERRY AUSTIN
Asst. Editor
STEPHANIE BUSCEMA
Editor
JOEY CAVALIERI
Colored by
LEE LOUGHRIDGE
The SPIRIT created by Will Eisner
I HAVE AN APPOINTMENT WITH MR. ARGOSY...BUT IT SHOULDN'T TAKE LONG! IF YOU'RE STILL AROUND WHEN I'M THROUGH...
SORRY... MY MOTHER WARNED ME ABOUT GUYS WHO WEAR MASKS AND AREN'T THE LONE RANGER...
Ah, SPIRIT! I'M ALWAYS LOOKING FOR THE PERSON WHO CAN HANDLE MY IMMEDIATE PROBLEM...
ARGOSY INSURANCE

SO AM I, MR. ARGOSY!

STOP LOOKING AT HER AND LOOK AT THIS PICTURE! IT'S OF MRS. EDNA OTIS--ONE OF THE RICHEST WOMEN IN THE COUNTRY!

MRS. OTIS HAS JEWELRY WORTH *MILLIONS*, WHICH SHE INSISTS ON *ACTUALLY WEARING!*

LET ME GUESS: A CLIENT OF YOURS AND SHE KEEPS GETTING ROBBED?

BINGO! LAST YEAR, SHE TOOK AN OCEAN CRUISE AND CLAIMED A VERY VALUABLE EMERALD AND DIAMOND NECKLACE FELL OVERBOARD!

HARD TO PROVE.

WHICH IS WHY WE HAD TO PAY OFF. WE THINK THE NECKLACE LATER "SURFACED" ON THE MARKET BUT RECUT AND WITH THE STONES IN OTHER SETTINGS.

WE HAD TO PAY OFF THE CLAIM. MRS. OTIS HAS LAWYERS.

AND NOW, THIS WOMAN IS TAKING *ANOTHER CRUISE!* AND SHE'S TAKING ALL HER JEWELRY ALONG WITH HER, SHE SAYS!

Uh, WOULDN'T IT BE A LITTLE *OBVIOUS* IF SHE LOST *ANOTHER* HEAVILY INSURED PIECE OVER THE RAIL?

OBVIOUS TO US? YES.

OBVIOUS TO A JUDGE OR JURY? YOU'D BE SURPRISED HOW RARELY THEY GIVE AN INSURANCE COMPANY THE BENEFIT OF THE DOUBT.

SPAT!

SOUNDS LIKE I NEED AN OCEAN VOYAGE! CAN YOU ARRANGE PASSAGE?

ALREADY ARRANGED! THE SHIP LEAVES TOMORROW MORNING!

MY SECRETARY CAN GIVE YOU EVERYTHING YOU NEED!

YES, I'M SURE SHE CAN.

ITINERARY... TICKETS... IS THERE ANYTHING ELSE I COULD HELP YOU WITH?

WELL, NOW THAT YOU MENTION IT...

DON'T YOU HAVE TO GO PACK YOUR SPARE HAT, SPIRIT?

Outside, Ebony is waiting-- with the meter off...

WHERE TO, BOSS?

HOME!

I HAVE TO PACK MY SPARE HAT!

PT082

LT 936

THEN, TOMORROW MORNING, I NEED YOU TO DRIVE ME TO THE PIER! I'M TAKING AN OCEAN VOYAGE!

HA! I KNEW YOU COULDN'T KEEP AWAY FROM MISS ELLEN!

ELLEN! I FORGOT! WHAT ARE THE ODDS SHE'LL BE ON THE SAME CRUISE?

THE WAY YOUR LUCK RUNS, I'D SAY ABOUT THE SAME AS THE ODDS OF ME HAVING VITO'S PIZZA FOR DINNER AND FALLING ASLEEP WATCHING LENO!

YOU TWO ARE LIKE A CAR WRECK AND A CROOKED LAWYER! WHEN YOU SEE ONE, THE OTHER'S NEVER FAR AWAY!

BON VOYAGE!

The next morning at Pier 19...

WELCOME ABOARD...RIGHT THIS WAY...YOU'RE IN STATEROOM 7 ON THE LIDO DECK...

CARIBBEAN QUEST

SO...WHAT IS THERE TO DO ON THIS OVERSIZED CANOE?

EAT...PLAY SHUFFLEBOARD...

THERE'S ONE *OTHER* THING, BUT I SEE YOU BROUGHT SOMEONE WITH YOU!

MAYBE I WAS WRONG. MAYBE ELLEN AND HER FRIENDS WON'T BE ON THIS SHIP TO COMPLICATE MY LIFE. MAYBE...

ELLEN DOLAN, CYNTHIA MORGAN AND LORI FIEDLER.

YOU'RE ON THE FIESTA DECK, LEVEL TWO...

MAYBE I'LL FLAP MY ARMS AND FLY TO THE MOON.

I'M *PURVIS*, THE CONTEST WINNER!

LET ME LOOK YOU UP...

DO YOU THINK THERE'LL BE ANY INTERESTING MEN ON THIS CRUISE?

THEY'LL *HAVE TO* BE BETTER THAN THE ONES I'M USUALLY AROUND!

I'VE NEVER BEEN ON A CRUISE SHIP BEFORE! IS IT TRUE ALL THE MEALS ARE *FREE*?

YES...BUT GIVEN THE SIZE OF THE STATEROOM THEY'VE ASSIGNED YOU, YOU MIGHT NOT WANT TO EAT *TOO* MUCH!

MRS. OTIS! A PLEASURE AS ALWAYS TO HAVE YOU ABOARD!

THANK YOU, SVEN! I ALMOST DIDN'T RETURN...

WHAT A NECKLACE! I'VE SEEN SMALLER ROCKS ON FLINTSTONES RERUNS!

AFTER THAT UNFORTUNATE ACCIDENT LAST TIME... WELL, WHAT'S DONE IS DONE!

MR. AND MRS. HAROLD DUPREE.

HEY, DID A GUY NAMED PURVIS GET ON BOARD YET?

YOU SHOULDN'T ASK ABOUT--

HEY, SHUT UP, WILL YA? I GOTTA KNOW.

NELSON PURVIS? JUST CHECKED HIM INTO THE STATEROOM NEXT TO YOURS. YOU KNOW HIM?

Uh, SORT OF. FRIEND OF A FRIEND... YOU KNOW.

THAT WAS STUPID. NOW, HE CAN CONNECT THE TWO OF YOU.

RELAX. THAT GUY CHECKS IN A THOUSAND PEOPLE A DAY. YOU THINK HE'S GOING TO REMEMBER ONE CONVERSATION?

GENTLEMEN? YOUR NAMES?

MR. CONRAD AND MR. CONRAD.

YEAH. WE'RE THE CONRAD BROTHERS.

THERE'S TWO GUYS WHO DON'T LOOK LIKE THEY BELONG ON THIS SHIP!

THOUGH COME TO THINK OF IT, THEY COULD BE THINKING THE SAME THING ABOUT ME.

THEY GOTTA HAVE A BAR ON THIS HEAP.

HI, NEIGHBOR!

AFTERNOON! HAVE A NICE CRUISE!

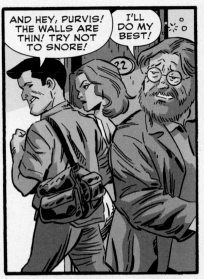

AND HEY, PURVIS! THE WALLS ARE THIN! TRY NOT TO SNORE!

I'LL DO MY BEST!

YOU IDIOT! WHY DON'T YOU JUST GET YOUR PICTURE TAKEN WITH HIM?

OW! WHAT'S WRONG?

WHAT'S WRONG IS YOU DON'T KNOW WHEN TO SHUT UP!

OKAY, OKAY!

IS THAT ELBOW OF YOURS REGISTERED AS A DANGEROUS WEAPON?

THERE'S SOMETHING *UNSETTLING* GOING ON HERE! I'M NOT SURE IF IT'S A CRIME IN PROGRESS OR AN EARLY ATTACK OF SEASICKNESS!

MAYBE IT'S THE APPROACH OF THAT PERSON I SEE COMING DOWN THE CORRIDOR!

THIS IS OUR SUITE.

THEY CALL THEM STATEROOMS!

I DON'T CARE WHAT IT'S CALLED AS LONG AS IT HAS A BED IN IT!

RIGHT ACROSS FROM ME! THIS IS SURE GOING TO MAKE THINGS UNCOMFORTABLE!

And so, the trip proceeds uneventfully...

Apart from one passenger polishing off the buffet almost single-handedly, nothing unusual occurs...

The Spirit keeps an eye on Mrs. Otis and her neck...

THAT THING SHE'S WEARING IS WORTH MORE THAN THE *ENTIRE* SHIP...

SHE JUST WALKS AROUND WITH IT ON... LIKE SHE'S ALMOST *DARING* SOMEONE TO STEAL IT...

SHE LOST THE LAST ONE ON THIS SHIP...

WHY ISN'T SHE MORE CAREFUL WITH IT? COULD SHE POSSIBLY--

Uh-oh.

THAT CABIN BOY WAS SO CUTE!

NOT YOUR TYPE.

BESIDES, I SAW HIM FIRST.

GOT TO STAY OUT OF *SIGHT*...

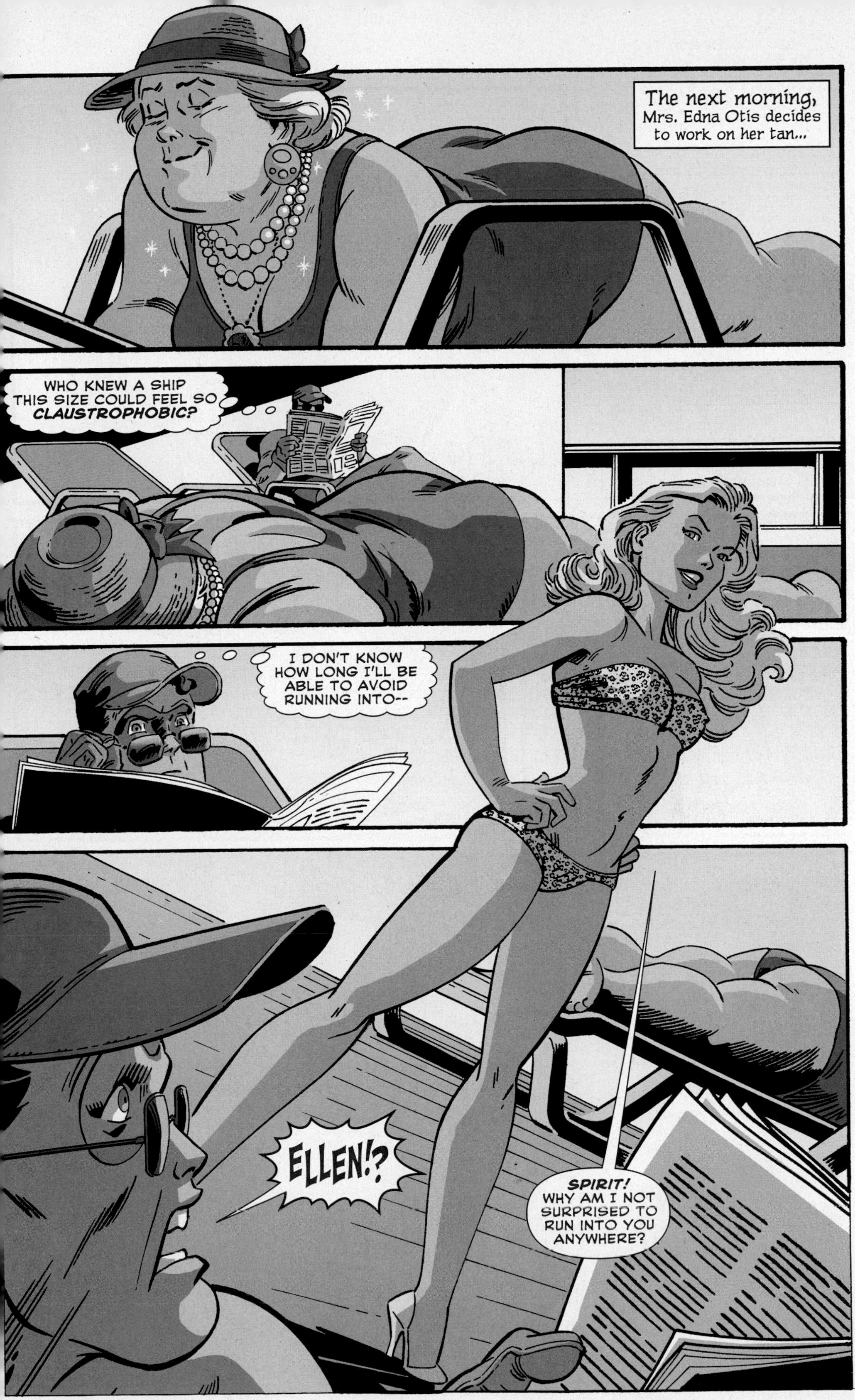
The next morning, Mrs. Edna Otis decides to work on her tan...
WHO KNEW A SHIP THIS SIZE COULD FEEL SO CLAUSTROPHOBIC?
I DON'T KNOW HOW LONG I'LL BE ABLE TO AVOID RUNNING INTO--
ELLEN!?
SPIRIT! WHY AM I NOT SURPRISED TO RUN INTO YOU ANYWHERE?

YOU FOLLOWED ME BECAUSE YOUR HEART COULDN'T *BEAR* FOR THE TWO OF US TO BE APART!

I DID? I COULDN'T?

I UNDERSTAND HOW *REPRESSED* YOU ARE, SPIRIT...HOW YOU SHY FROM EVEN THE *SLIGHTEST* PUBLIC DISPLAY OF PASSION OR AFFECTION...

YOU SHOULD BE MORE LIKE THAT MAN OVER THERE WITH HIS WIFE! YOU DON'T WANT PEOPLE TO SEE THE REAL *YOU!*

I DON'T HAVE THAT PROBLEM!

THEN WHY DO YOU WEAR A MASK EVERYWHERE YOU GO?

IT'S HARD TO EXPLAIN...

I'M SORRY! I NEED TO KEEP AN EYE ON SOMEONE!

WHERE'D SHE GO?

NEVER MIND HER, WHOEVER "SHE" IS! I'M RIGHT HERE FOR YOU, SPIRIT!

OH! THERE SHE IS!

HOW'D I *MISS* HER?

YOU'D RATHER LOOK AT *HER* THAN *ME?*

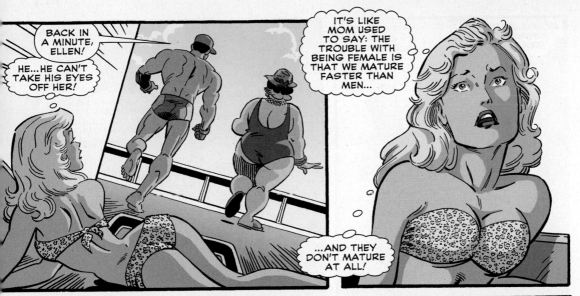

BACK IN A MINUTE, ELLEN!

HE...HE CAN'T TAKE HIS EYES OFF HER!

IT'S LIKE MOM USED TO SAY: THE TROUBLE WITH BEING FEMALE IS THAT WE MATURE FASTER THAN MEN...

...AND THEY DON'T MATURE AT ALL!

The Spirit follows Mrs. Otis back to her cabin...

SHE'S SAFE IN THERE FOR NOW! MAYBE I SHOULD GO PUT THINGS RIGHT WITH ELLEN...

TROUBLE IS, I DON'T KNOW WHAT "RIGHT" IS!

HEY, WHAT'S WITH THE MASK, FELLA? IS THIS TRICK OR TREAT?

NO, AND IT'S NOT *NEW YEAR'S EVE*, EITHER! I THINK YOU'VE HAD A BIT *TOO MUCH* TO DRINK...LIKE A COUPLE GALLONS!

CAN'T HAVE TOO MUCH! NOT WHEN IT'S *FREE!*

YOU KNOW THEY GIVE YOU ALL YOU CAN EAT *AND* DRINK?

LOVELY. HEY, TRY NOT TO BREATHE UPWARDS. YOU'LL MELT THE SMOKE DETECTORS!

I NEVER WON ANYTHING BEFORE! 'COURSE, I NEVER ENTERED A CONTEST BEFORE!

FUNNY THING... I DON'T REMEMBER ENTERING *THIS ONE* BUT I MUST'VE ON ACCOUNT OF HERE I AM!

WELL, HE KNOWS WHERE HE IS. THAT'S A GOOD SIGN.

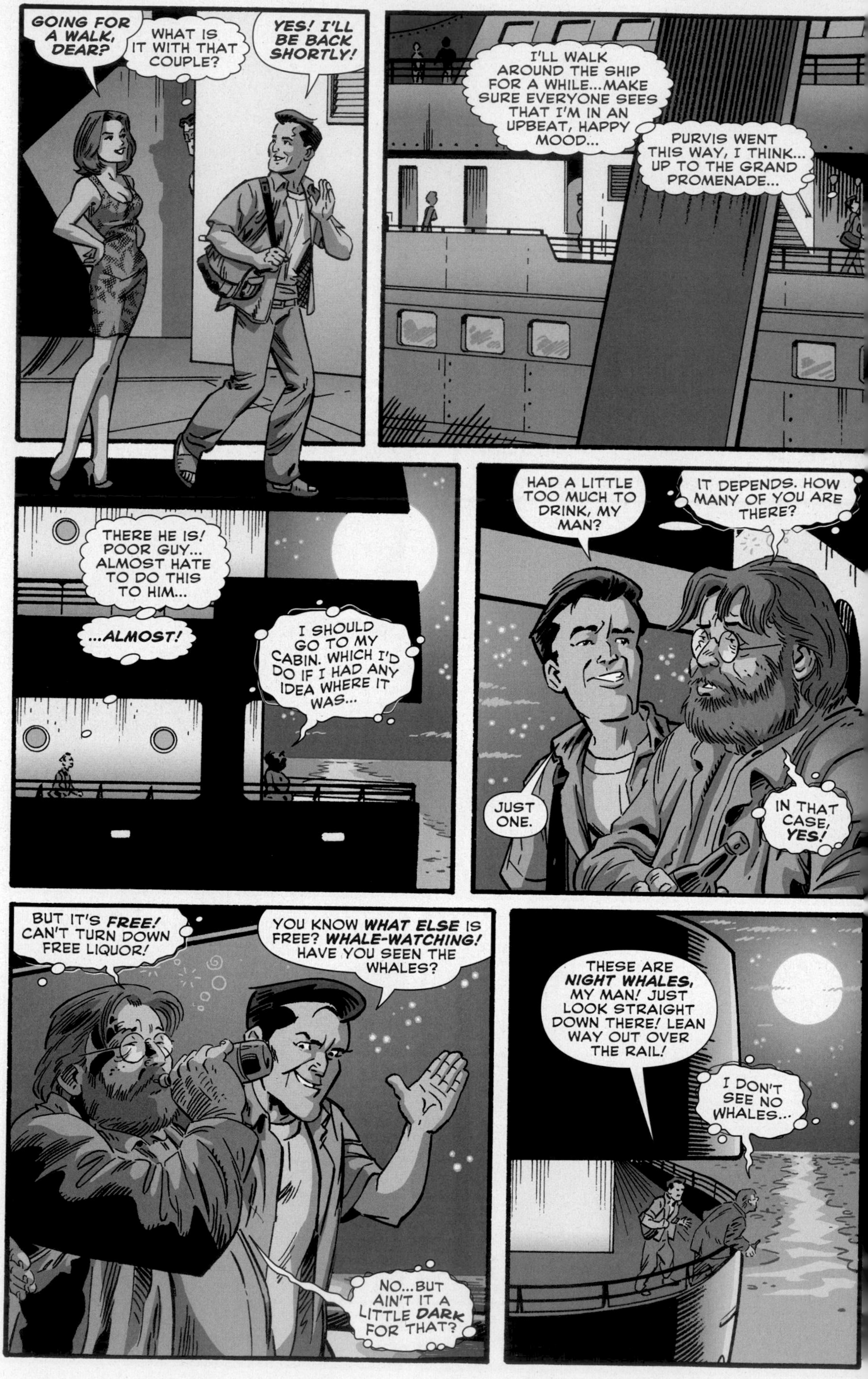

GOING FOR A WALK, DEAR?
WHAT IS IT WITH THAT COUPLE?
YES! I'LL BE BACK SHORTLY!
I'LL WALK AROUND THE SHIP FOR A WHILE...MAKE SURE EVERYONE SEES THAT I'M IN AN UPBEAT, HAPPY MOOD...
PURVIS WENT THIS WAY, I THINK... UP TO THE GRAND PROMENADE...
THERE HE IS! POOR GUY... ALMOST HATE TO DO THIS TO HIM...
...ALMOST!
I SHOULD GO TO MY CABIN. WHICH I'D DO IF I HAD ANY IDEA WHERE IT WAS...
HAD A LITTLE TOO MUCH TO DRINK, MY MAN?
IT DEPENDS. HOW MANY OF YOU ARE THERE?
JUST ONE.
IN THAT CASE, YES!
BUT IT'S FREE! CAN'T TURN DOWN FREE LIQUOR!
YOU KNOW WHAT ELSE IS FREE? WHALE-WATCHING! HAVE YOU SEEN THE WHALES?
NO...BUT AIN'T IT A LITTLE DARK FOR THAT?
THESE ARE NIGHT WHALES, MY MAN! JUST LOOK STRAIGHT DOWN THERE! LEAN WAY OUT OVER THE RAIL!
I DON'T SEE NO WHALES...

NICE NIGHT! BUT I SHOULD GET BACK DOWN AND KEEP AN EYE ON MRS. OTIS AND HER STATEROOM...

HELP! MY JEWELS!

...ESPECIALLY *NOW!*

THOSE BOYS! COMING OUT OF HER CABIN!

MY NECKLACE! MY BEAUTIFUL, PRECIOUS NECKLACE! AND ALL MY JEWELRY!

SOMETHING ABOUT THIS DOESN'T SEEM RIGHT...

...BUT I CAN WORRY ABOUT THAT *LATER!*

THEY'RE ON THE LIDO DECK *BELOW--*

--WHICH IS WHERE I OUGHT TO BE!

HI, SAILOR!

I BELIEVE YOU GUYS TOOK SOMETHING THAT DOESN'T BELONG TO YOU!

WE DIDN'T TAKE NOTHIN', FELLA!

BUT YOU'RE GONNA TAKE *THIS*!

THIS DOESN'T MAKE A LOT OF SENSE! WE'RE IN THE MIDDLE OF THE OCEAN! WHERE DO THEY THINK THEY'RE GOING TO RUN TO?

Uh-oh. HE'S PULLING OUT A GUN!

NO! HE WAS PULLING OUT MRS. OTIS'S JEWELS! AND THEY JUST WENT *OVERBOARD*!

OKAY, SO YOU GOT US! BUT *WHAT* ARE YOU GONNA ARREST US FOR? NOT THAT YOU EVEN GOT *JURISDICTION* OUT HERE!

SOMEONE DOES! AND THEY'LL CHARGE YOU FOR STEALING MRS. OTIS'S JEWELRY AND NECKLACE!

WHAT JEWELR AND NECKLAC I DON'T SEE A JEWELRY AND NECKLACE!

Before the Spirit can ponder that, a cry rings out...

MAN OVERBOARD!

WHAT? WHO?

Swiftly, he ties up the Conrad boys...

NOT GONNA DO YOU ANY GOOD, COP...OR WHATEVER YOU ARE! YOU AIN'T GOT A *SHRED OF PROOF* WE COMMITTED ANY CRIME!

WE'LL SEE ABOUT THAT-- *LATER!*

IT WAS *MR. DUPREE?* ARE YOU SURE?

ABSOLUTELY! I WAS LEANING OVER THE RAIL AND I LOST MY BALANCE! HE GRABBED ME AND SAVED MY LIFE--

--AND SOMEHOW, *HE SLIPPED* AND FELL *OVERBOARD!*

They search...

For hours, they search...

But there is no trace of William H. Dupree...

DO SOMETHING! MY POOR HUSBAND! DROWNED IN THE OCEAN LIKE THAT!

WE'RE DOING EVERYTHING HUMANLY POSSIBLE!

THE WATER'S DEEP HERE! VERY TREACHEROUS!

MY LIFE IS OVER WITHOUT HIM! BILL MEANT EVERYTHING TO ME IN THE WORLD!

MAN, SHE REALLY MUST HAVE LOVED HIM!

Uh-huh...

MY TIPSY FRIEND SEEMS TO HAVE SOBERED UP IN A HURRY! HE DOESN'T EVEN *SMELL* OF ALCOHOL!

SO YOU DON'T THINK THERE'S ANY CHANCE OF FINDING HIS BODY?

OUT HERE? HIGHLY UNLIKELY.

Minutes *later*, in the ship's business center...

LET'S SEE IF THAT "INSTANT MESSAGING" ADDRESS FOR MR. ARGOSY WILL WORK...

HOPE HE'S UP AND AT HIS COMPUTER...

Ten minutes later...

YEP! AND INSURED BY THE SAME COMPANY!

LET'S SEE IF I CAN WRAP UP *ACT ONE* OF THIS...

MRS. OTIS? DO YOU HAVE A MOMENT TO IDENTIFY SOMEONE FOR ME?

OH, WHAT DOES IT MATTER? I'LL NEVER SEE MY PRECIOUS JEWELS AGAIN!

BUT IF YOU MUST, BRING THEM IN!

HERE THEY ARE-- THE MEN WHO STOLE YOUR JEWELRY!

THEM? OH, I'M AFRAID YOU'RE *MISTAKEN!* I DIDN'T GET A GOOD LOOK AT THE MEN WHO ROBBED ME BUT I'M SURE IT WASN'T *THESE TWO!*

SHE'S "SURE IT WASN'T *THESE TWO!*"

SO NO STOLEN JEWELS AND NO WITNESS! LOOKS LIKE YOU'VE GOTTA LET US GO!

LET YOU GO?

NOW THEN...

STILL WANT ME TO LET YOU GO?

ALL RIGHT, ALL RIGHT! SHE HIRED US TO THROW THE JEWELS OVER!

BUT NOT THE *REAL* JEWELS, I ASSUME...

NO...CHEAP IMITATIONS! SHE SOLD THE *REAL* ONES! TO SOME GUY FROM SOUTH AMERICA! I DON'T KNOW HIS NAME! *I SWEAR!*

Within minutes...

WHAT DO YOU THINK THEY'LL CHARGE US WITH? MRS. OTIS-- SHE WAS THE ONE COMMITTING INSURANCE FRAUD!

THEY'LL FIND SOMETHING. THEY *ALWAYS* FIND SOMETHING.

While on the fiesta deck...

I NEED TO FIND THAT MRS. DUPREE...

SPIRIT, DARLING! YOU CAME LOOKING FOR ME SO WE COULD BE TOGETHER?

WELL, uh, NO...

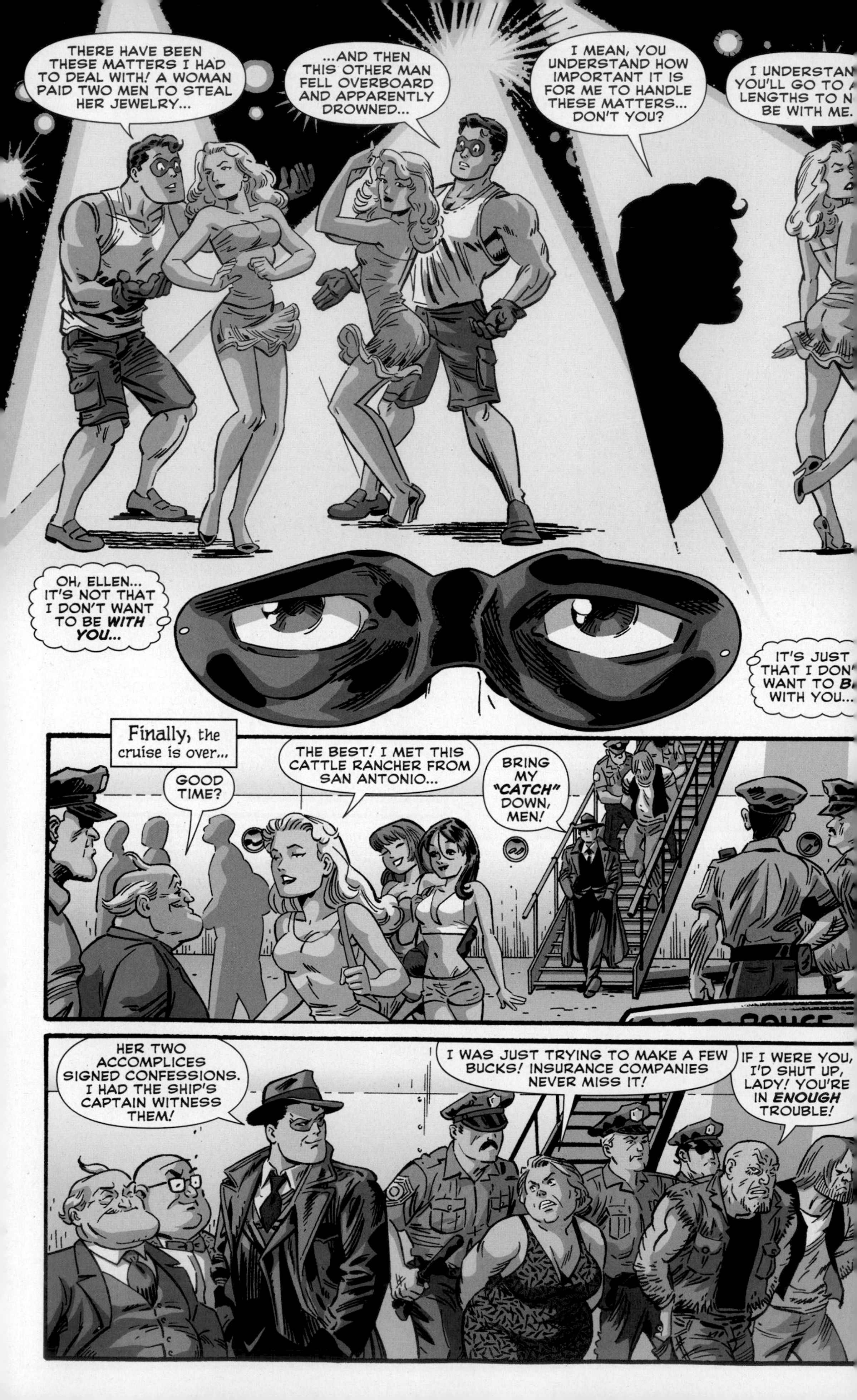

THERE HAVE BEEN THESE MATTERS I HAD TO DEAL WITH! A WOMAN PAID TWO MEN TO STEAL HER JEWELRY...
...AND THEN THIS OTHER MAN FELL OVERBOARD AND APPARENTLY DROWNED...
I MEAN, YOU UNDERSTAND HOW IMPORTANT IT IS FOR ME TO HANDLE THESE MATTERS... DON'T YOU?
I UNDERSTAN YOU'LL GO TO LENGTHS TO N BE WITH ME.
OH, ELLEN... IT'S NOT THAT I DON'T WANT TO BE *WITH* YOU...
IT'S JUST THAT I DON' WANT TO B WITH YOU...
Finally, the cruise is over...
GOOD TIME?
THE BEST! I MET THIS CATTLE RANCHER FROM SAN ANTONIO...
BRING MY *"CATCH"* DOWN, MEN!
HER TWO ACCOMPLICES SIGNED CONFESSIONS. I HAD THE SHIP'S CAPTAIN WITNESS THEM!
I WAS JUST TRYING TO MAKE A FEW BUCKS! INSURANCE COMPANIES NEVER MISS IT!
IF I WERE YOU, I'D SHUT UP, LADY! YOU'RE IN *ENOUGH* TROUBLE!

I TAKE IT THAT'S THE WOMAN YOU WROTE ME ABOUT! I CHECKED AND THE LIFE INSURANCE POLICY ON HER HUSBAND IS WORTH 2.5 MILLION!

ABOUT WHAT I GUESSED.

SPIRIT...WHAT WAS THAT "OTHER MATTER" YOU TOLD ME YOU WERE LOOKING INTO?

LATER, COMMISSIONER. LET'S JUST SAY I HAVE A LITTLE MORE INVESTIGATING TO DO ON IT!

Nelson Purvis returns to his old apartment in the not-so-nice part of town...

HELLO? MR. PURVIS?

OH... HELLO!

SOMETHING WRONG? YOU WALKED RIGHT BY LIKE YOU DIDN'T EVEN KNOW ME!

OH...SORRY! I'M JUST PREOCCUPIED...I'VE DECIDED TO MAKE SOME CHANGES IN MY LIFE!

THAT'S RIGHT... A ONE-WAY TICKET TO PARIS! MY NAME IS PURVIS...NELSON PURVIS...

NO, IT ISN'T...

IT'S DUPREE... WILLIAM DUPREE--THE MAN WHO'S GOING TO PRISON AND MAYBE WORSE FOR THE MURDER OF NELSON PURVIS!

DOLAN? YEAH, IT'S ME. REMEMBER THAT "OTHER MATTER" I MENTIONED? WELL, YOU'RE GOING TO NEED A *CELL* FOR IT! NO, MAKE THAT *TWO* CELLS!

WHAT IN GOD'S NAME ARE YOU DOING *HERE*? SOMEONE COULD HAVE SEEN YOU COME INTO THE BUILDING, YOU IDIOT!

DON'T YOU HAVE *ANY* CONCEPT OF HOW THIS IS SUPPOSED TO WORK? NO ONE IS TO KNOW THAT WE HAVE ANY CONNECTION! THAT'S WHY WE PICKED A STRANGER LIKE PURVIS...SOMEONE WHO COULDN'T BE LINKED TO US...

...SOMEONE WHO COULDN'T BE LINKED TO *ANYONE*!

NOW, GIVE ME A KISS AND GET BACK TO HIS PLACE! MAKE IT LOOK LIKE THERE'S NOTHING SUSPICIOUS ABOUT HIS SUDDEN DECISION TO MOVE OVERSEAS!

WAIT... LET ME GET THIS JUNK OFF YOU! I WANT TO KISS *YOU*, BILL!

I'M AFRAID YOU'RE GOING TO HAVE TO COME DOWNTOWN TO DO THAT.

HE DID IT, NOT *ME*! IT WAS *HIS* IDEA! *HE* WAS THE ONE WHO PUSHED THE OLD LOSER OVERBOARD! I COULD TURN STATE'S EVIDENCE!

THANKS...BUT I REALLY DON'T THINK THAT'LL BE NECESSARY!

I WANT A LAWYER.

IF I WERE YOU, I'D WANT A WHOLE LOT OF THEM!

THEY SCOUTED PURVIS FOR MONTHS. MRS. DUPREE WORKED AT A CLINIC SO SHE HAD ACCESS TO RECORDS!

THEY HAD TO PICK SOMEONE WITH *NO* FAMILY, *NO* FRIENDS...AND *NO* REASON NOT TO PICK UP AND MOVE SOMEWHERE NEW!

NICE WORK, SPIRIT... ON THE JEWELRY SCAM, ON THE MURDER...

...AND FROM WHAT ELLEN TELLS ME, A FINE JOB OF AVOIDING HER IN EVERY ONE OF THE TWENTY-THREE CITIES!

IT'S NOT THAT I DON'T LIKE YOUR DAUGHTER, SIR! IT'S JUST THAT ON THE SHIP... WITH TWO CASES TO JUGGLE, I WAS VERY BUSY...

NOW THAT I'M NOT, I'LL GIVE HER A CALL SOME DAY...SEE IF SHE WANTS TO GO HEAR SOME AUTHENTIC JAZZ OR SOMETHING...

DID I HEAR YOU SAY YOU WERE *NOT BUSY*, SPIRIT?

JUST IN TIME FOR US TO GO SKIING IN THE MOUNTAINS! BETTER GET YOUR FUR-LINED *MASK!* IT'S GOING TO BE CHILLY!

I WOULDN'T BE THE LEAST BIT SURPRISED!

THE END

Art by Paul Smith & Lee Loughridge

the dangers of hanging 'round Commissioner Dolan's office...

GOT AN ASSIGNMENT FOR YOU, SPIRIT.

DON'T TELL ME. **LET ME GUESS.** SUPERMODELS, FINE WINES, FOUR-STAR HOTELS AND NO CHANCE OF ME GETTING KILLED OR BEATEN UP?

FOR A GOOD DETECTIVE, YOU'RE A ROTTEN GUESSER.

HI, ELLEN! WHERE'S YOUR FATHER SENDING ME?

EGYPT. AT THE REQUEST OF THE U.S. CUSTOMS DEPARTMENT.

DON'T I GET A KISS FIRST?

ON THE **CHEEK?** HOW CHARMING AND NONCOMMITTAL!

MAYBE YOU SHOULD TAKE ME WITH YOU SO WE COULD GET *"BETTER ACQUAINTED!"*

Uh...THAT WOULDN'T WORK. WOULD IT, DOLAN?

NO. YOU'LL NEED TO PUT ALL YOUR ATTENTION ON THE **MUMMIES!** THERE ARE AN EVEN **DOZEN** OF THEM AND YOU'LL GUARD THEM ON THEIR WAY TO THE **MUSEUM** HERE.

BODYGUARD TO A BUNCH OF MUMMIES, *huh?* I'VE HAD WORSE JOBS!

WE'VE HAD SOME WONDERFUL TIMES TOGETHER, HAVEN'T WE? DON'T YOU REMEMBER THAT GREAT LITTLE *ITALIAN* RESTAURANT WITH THE CALAMARI FRITTA YOU LIKED SO MUCH?

SURE...

IT HAD THAT GREAT VIEW WHERE WE COULD LOOK OUT AND SEE ALL OF *ROME!*

I MEANT THE RESTAURANT OVER ON 9th STREET! I'VE **NEVER BEEN** TO ROME!

BUT YOU WERE THERE ONCE WHEN P'GELL WAS THERE...

NO, I **MEANT** THE RESTAURANT ON 9th STREET!

YOUR MUMMIES ARE WAITING FOR YOU, MR. SPIRIT! I'M SURE YOU'LL GET ALONG FINE WITH COLD, LIFELESS BODIES.

I DON'T BLAME HER. I WOULDN'T HAVE FORGIVEN ME, EITHER.

AT LEAST I'M SPARING HER WAITING IN *THIS LINE*...

I REMEMBER WHEN YOU COULD JUST GET ON THE PLANE AND GO! THEY DIDN'T PUT ON THIS WHOLE SHOW, PRETENDING THEY WERE MAKING US SAFER...

TAKE YOUR SHOES OFF AND THROW AWAY ANY DRINKING WATER.

THEY PUT ME THROUGH ALL THIS AND NO ONE EVEN NOTICES THAT I'M WEARING A MASK.

WHAT'S THAT YOU'RE CONCEALING UNDER YOUR DRESS, MA'AM?

I BELIEVE IT'S CALLED A FETUS.

THESE MUMMIES MUST BE PRETTY VALUABLE IF THE MUSEUM THINKS THEY NEED A *POLICE ESCORT* TO THE U.S. THE QUESTION IS *WHY ME?*

I KNOW AS MUCH ABOUT MUMMIES AS I KNOW ABOUT TALKING TO WOMEN...

ALL I KNOW IS WHAT I SAW IN BAD HORROR MOVIES. WHEN YOU'RE TRAPPED IN THE TOMB WITH THEM, THEY HAVE A TENDENCY TO COME BACK TO LIFE...

HOPE THAT DOESN'T HAPPEN...

I WOULDN'T WANT TO GO ALL THE WAY TO EGYPT AND FIND MYSELF IN THE MIDDLE OF AN *ABBOTT AND COSTELLO* MOVIE...

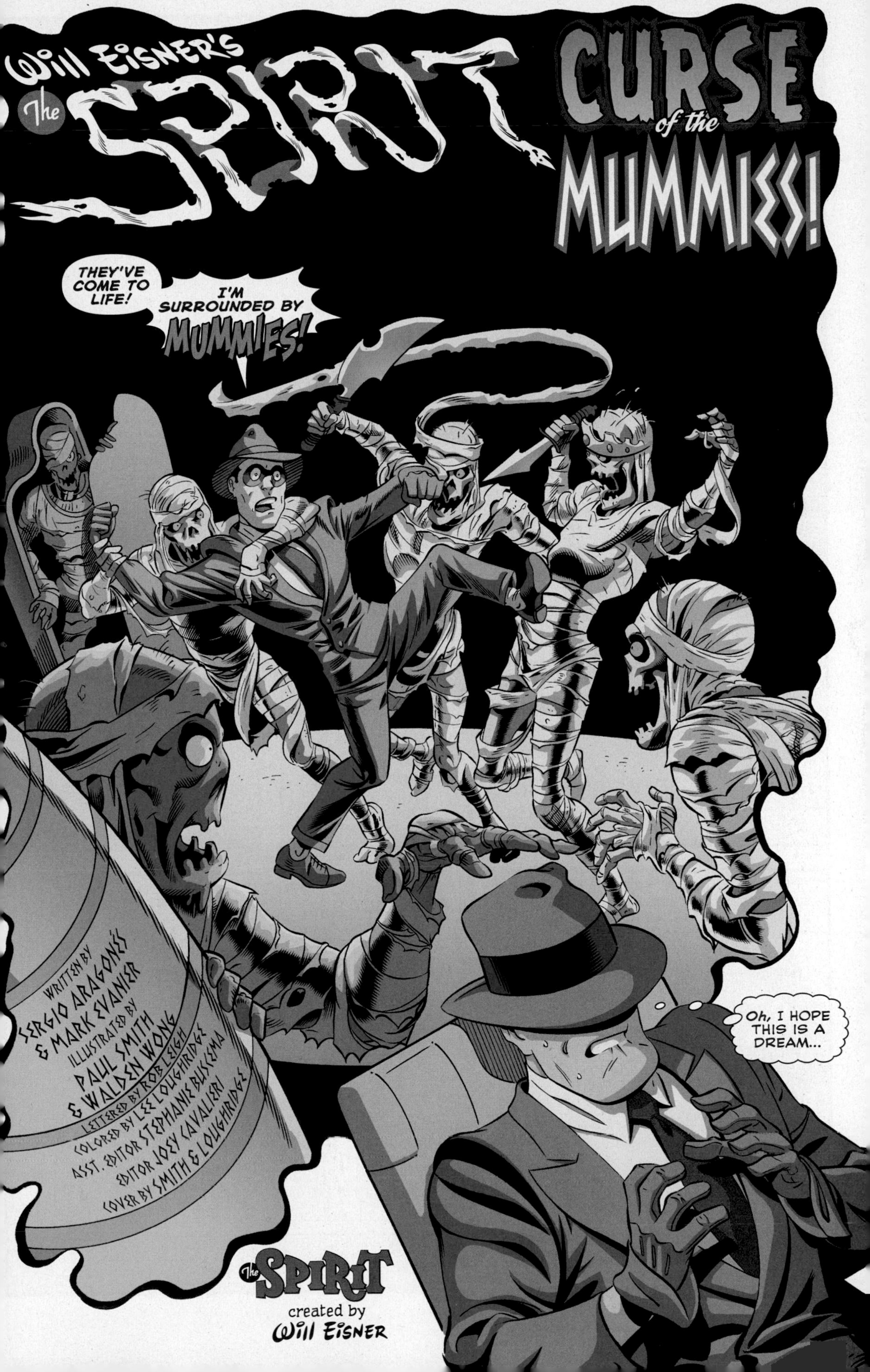
WILL EISNER'S
The SPIRIT
CURSE of the MUMMIES!
THEY'VE COME TO LIFE!
I'M SURROUNDED BY MUMMIES!
Oh, I HOPE THIS IS A DREAM...
WRITTEN BY SERGIO ARAGONÉS & MARK EVANIER
ILLUSTRATED BY PAUL SMITH & WALDEN WONG
LETTERED BY ROB LEIGH
COLORED BY LEE LOUGHRIDGE
ASST. EDITOR STEPHANIE BUSCEMA
EDITOR JOEY CAVALIERI
COVER BY SMITH & LOUGHRIDGE
The SPIRIT created by WILL EISNER

IT WAS. FUNNY HOW YOU KNOW IT'S A DREAM WHILE YOU'RE DREAMING IT--

--BUT IT'S STILL A RELIEF TO WAKE UP AND FIND OUT FOR SURE YOU WERE DREAMING, JUST IN CASE YOU WERE DREAMING YOU WERE DREAMING...

LOOKS LIKE WE'RE ABOUT TO LAND IN *EGYPT*.

EITHER THAT OR THE PILOT MISSED A LEFT TURN AT ALBUQUERQUE AND THAT'S *LAS VEGAS!*

MUSEUM OF ANTIQUITIES, PLEASE.

I WILL DO MY BEST, SAYYID. BUT THE TRAFFIC, IT IS VERY BAD DUE TO POLICE IN THE AREA.

ANY IDEA *WHY* THERE ARE POLICE IN THE AREA?

SOMETHING ABOUT MUMMIES BEING STOLEN!

SOUNDS LIKE THEY NEEDED A GOOD BODYGUARD.

HERE. KEEP THE CHANGE.

YOU WOULD NOT HAPPEN TO HAVE MONEY THAT IS NOT AMERICAN, WOULD YOU?

THAT IS **THE SPIRIT!** LET HIM PAST THE BLOCKADE IF YOU WILL!

THE PERKS OF WEARING A MASK.

SPIRIT, IT IS SO GOOD OF YOU TO COME! WE ARE WELL AWARE OF YOUR EXPLOITS AND COMMISSIONER DOLAN HIGHLY RECOMMENDED YOU FOR THIS MATTER.

ANYTHING TO GET ME OUT OF THE COUNTRY.

FROM WHAT I HEAR, I'M A LITTLE LATE. YOU ARE MR. AYAD, CORRECT?

CORRECT! AS YOU HAVE HEARD, THE MUMMIES HAVE BEEN STOLEN, BUT YOU NEED NOT CONCERN YOURSELF...

THE MATTER IS IN THE CAPABLE HANDS OF INSPECTOR MUHAD RADO, OUR CHIEF INVESTIGATOR.

A PLEASURE, MR. RADO.

THE PLEASURE IS MINE, SIR...

LONG HAVE I HEARD TALES OF THE SPIRIT... FROM LAW ENFORCEMENT OFFICIALS AND ALSO WITH MEN IN OUR PRISONS WHO HAVE CROSSED YOUR PATH!

WELL, MAYBE I CAN HELP HERE. COULD I SEE PHOTOS OF THE MUMMIES? AND I'D LIKE TO SEE THE ROOM FROM WHICH THEY WERE TAKEN...

THAT WILL NOT BE NECESSARY, SPIRIT. I APOLOGIZE YOU HAVE COME SO FAR, BUT AS I SAID, THE MATTER IS IN THE HANDS OF INSPECTOR RADO!

NO OFFENSE, MY SIR, BUT YOU ARE WITHOUT JURISDICTION HERE... OR KNOWLEDGE OF OUR CULTURE AND THIS CITY...

PLEASE, MR. AYAD! I AM WITHOUT LEADS AT THE MOMENT, AND IT WOULD BE FOOLISH TO WASTE A VALUABLE RESOURCE SUCH AS THE SPIRIT! ALLOW HIM TO ASSIST!

IF YOU WISH! BUT HE DOES NOT HAVE JURISDICTION...

I DON'T HAVE JURISDICTION *ANYWHERE*, SIR. SOMEHOW, THAT'S NEVER STOPPED ME!

I'D BE GLAD TO HELP YOU FIND YOUR MUMMIES!

THEY SAY THAT *WHATEVER* ONE WISHES TO FIND, IT CAN BE FOUND IN A MARKETPLACE IN CAIRO! EVEN, I HOPE, *LOST MUMMIES.*

THIS PLACE LOOKS LIKE *COSTCO* WITH VEILS! SO WERE THESE MUMMIES PARTICULARLY VALUABLE? IS THERE A PRICE GUIDE ON MUMMIES?

THAT IS THE PUZZLING PART, MY FRIEND. THEY WERE NOT OF ROYALTY OR LINEAGE.

THEY WERE JUST THE MUMMIFIED REMAINS OF TWELVE PEASANTS... PROBABLY PRIESTS OR MERCHANTS!

WELL, *SOMEONE* MUST HAVE WANTED THEM.

ANTIQU

But trader after trader has heard nothing...

IF ANYONE APPROACHES ME ABOUT THEM, I WILL OF COURSE NOTIFY YOU, INSPECTOR.

THANK YOU. AND SPREAD THE WORD TO *OTHER MERCHANTS,* IF YOU PLEASE.

I SAW THAT MOVIE.

THE MUMMIES ARE OF LITTLE VALUE HERE IN EGYPT. THEY WOULD COMMAND A *SLIGHTLY* HIGHER PRICE IN OTHER COUNTRIES... BUT SMUGGLING TWELVE MUMMIES OUT OF THE COUNTRY WOULD HARDLY BE EASY, HARDLY WORTH THE TROUBLE.

WHICH LEAVES US BACK WONDERING WHY ANYONE WOULD STEAL THEM.

THAT IS A QUESTION MOST BAFFLING, MY FRIEND. *TELL ME* WHAT YOU ARE THINKING!

I'M THINKING THAT'S THE *UGLIEST LAMP* I'VE EVER SEEN IN MY LIFE.

WHERE DO I GET ONE FOR DOLAN?

Next stop: the customs office at Cairo International Airport...

INSPECTOR ADUZ AND HIS MEN ARE VERY GOOD AT CATCHING SMUGGLERS!

SO YOU'RE THINKING THEY COULD SPOT SOME GUY TRYING TO GET OUT OF THE COUNTRY WITH TWELVE MUMMIES IN HIS PANTS...

THERE IS *NO WAY* THEY COULD BE SMUGGLED OUT OF EGYPT! NOT SOMETHING OF *THAT SIZE*!

NOT ONLY THE AIRPORT BUT ALL THE SEAPORTS, TRAIN STATIONS AND TRUCK STOPS ARE PROPERLY SCRUTINIZED.

THANK YOU, SIR.

HE'S RIGHT. NONE OF THIS MAKES SENSE... *INCLUDING* THE FACT THAT I WAS ASKED TO GUARD THESE WORTHLESS MUMMIES.

I AM HOPING YOU ARE NOT AS STYMIED AS IT WOULD APPEAR.

WELL, I HATE TO DASH YOUR HOPES BUT...

DOLAN SAID I WAS REQUESTED BY THE CUSTOMS DEPARTMENT. SO PERHAPS SOMEONE WAS SMUGGLING SOMETHING *INSIDE* THE MUMMIES--?

THAT OCCURRED TO ME AS WELL...

APPARENTLY, THEY RECEIVED SOME SORT OF TIP...CHATTER THEY PICKED UP ALONG A PRISON GRAPEVINE. BUT HOW AND TO WHAT END?

LET ME OFF UP HERE, DRIVER!

I THINK I'D LIKE TO WALK THE REST OF THE WAY TO MY HOTEL... DRINK IN SOME OF THE LOCAL COLOR...

MAKE CERTAIN THAT IS ALL YOU DRINK IN, MY FRIEND! I SHALL CALL YOU WHEN I KNOW MORE.

THAT IS *HIM!* WHAT IS *HE* DOING HERE IN EGYPT?

I HAD BEST TELL THE BOSS RIGHT AWAY!

I AM JUST THE MESSENGER.

HERE? *IN CAIRO?* WHEREVER I VENTURE, *HE* TURNS UP TO RUIN MY PLANS!

I REPEAT: I AM JUST THE MESSENGER, OCTOPUS! DO NOT HARM ME.

WELL, HE WON'T RUIN *THIS ONE!* THIS ONE IS *TOO PERFECT* FOR ANYONE TO RUIN... EVEN THE SPIRIT! AM I RIGHT?

YOU ARE RIGHT, OCTOPUS!

GOOD. NOW, FIND THE SPIRIT AND *KILL HIM!* JUST TO MAKE CERTAIN!

THE MUMMIES ARE READY, OCTOPUS!

EXCELLENT! NOW, DELIVER THEM BACK TO THE MUSEUM AS WE PLANNED!

THE SPIRIT WILL *NEVER* FIGURE THIS ONE OUT!

For a time, that seems like a fair prediction...

SORRY TO INTERRUPT YOU, KIND SIR...

NO, I WAS JUST SITTING HERE WITH NO IDEA WHAT'S GOING ON...

DO YOU HAVE SOMETHING FOR ME?

YOU ARE LOOKING FOR MUMMIES, I UNDERSTAND. WELL, COME WITH ME AND I SHALL TAKE YOU TO MUMMIES.

In a shop several blocks away...

HERE IS WHAT YOU ARE SEEKING, GOOD SIR...

MUMMIES.

...FOR EVERY TASTE, EVERY OCCASION! I HAVE TALL MUMMIES, SHORT MUMMIES, MUMMIES IN VARIOUS COLORS, MUMMIES WITH WI-FI INTERNET CAPABILITY...

OH, GREAT. I FOUND "MUMMIES 'R US!"

IN THE BACK, I HAVE A MUMMY ROCK BAND! MANY WESTERNERS SAY IT REMINDS THEM OF SOMETHING CALLED "THE ROLLING STONES!"

IF YOU ARE SHORT ON SPACE, I HAVE MUMMY MIDGETS...

CRASH

MY MUMMIES! DO NOT HURT MY MUMMIES!

CALL THE POLICE! I DON'T WANT TO END UP AS DEAD AS YOUR INVENTORY HERE!

IF THEY'RE TRYING TO KILL ME, I MUST BE GETTING CLOSE TO SOMETHING!

WISH I KNEW WHAT!

BLAMM BLABLAM

ALL RIGHT, *TALK!* WHO ARE YOU WORKING FOR? WHAT DO YOU KNOW ABOUT THE MISSING MUMMIES?

I'M NOT HEARING ANY ANSWERS OUT OF YOU BOYS! *COME ON!*

ONE OF YOU...SAY *SOMETHING!*

MY MUMMIES! MY BEAUTIFUL, DECREPIT MUMMIES!

WE WILL TAKE OVER, SPIRIT!

HEY, THIS PLACE IS FULL OF MUMMIES!

RADO! I TAKE IT NONE OF THESE ARE THE MISSING MUMMIES!

THESE ARE ALL STAGE PROPS! BUT WE DO NOT HAVE TO WORRY ABOUT THE MISSING MUMMIES ANYMORE!

I KNOW THESE MEN, INSPECTOR RADO! THEY ARE TOO AFRAID OF WHOEVER HIRED THEM TO TELL US ANYTHING!

WHY, PRAY TELL, DO WE NOT HAVE TO WORRY ABOUT THE MISSING MUMMIES?

BECAUSE THEY HAVE BEEN *RETURNED!* I WILL TAKE YOU TO THEM!

Two hours earlier, the errant mummies were found outside the Museum of Antiquities...

ANY IDEA HOW THEY GOT HERE? AND DON'T SAY, "THEY TOOK A LEFT TURN AT THE SPHINX!"

NO IDEA. A GUARD JUST FOUND THEM.

ANY SIGN OF DAMAGE?

NO. IN FACT, IT LOOKS LIKE WHOEVER "BORROWED" THEM DUSTED THEM OFF! HAVE YOU ANY THOUGHTS?

JUST ONE. THE U.S. CUSTOMS PEOPLE THOUGHT SMUGGLERS WERE SOMEHOW INTERESTED IN THESE MUMMIES! THE IDEA COULD HAVE BEEN TO USE THEM TO SNEAK SOMETHING IN!

YOU THINK THEY HID SOMETHING IN THE MUMMIES WHEN THEY HAD THEM?

MAYBE. IT'S NOT LIKE THE CUSTOMS PEOPLE ARE GOING TO STRIP-SEARCH TWELVE MUMMIES WHEN THEY ENTER THE COUNTRY.

THAT WOULD BE EASY TO DETECT. WE HAVE X-RAYS WE USE TO SCAN THE CORPSES FOR JEWELRY WITHOUT DISTURBING THE WRAPPINGS!

WE WILL DO IT AT ONCE!

But...

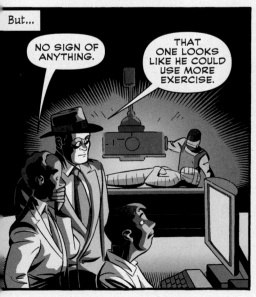

NO SIGN OF ANYTHING.

THAT ONE LOOKS LIKE HE COULD USE MORE EXERCISE.

THERE IS NO REASON NOW NOT TO SHIP THE MUMMIES TO YOUR AMERICA, ESPECIALLY WITH YOU ACCOMPANYING THEM.

RIGHT. BUT YOU KEEP ON DIGGING FROM YOUR END AND LET ME KNOW IF YOU FIND OUT ANYTHING.

I HOPE THE MUMMIES DON'T HAVE BETTER SEATS ON THE PLANE THAN I DO.

The next day, back in Central City...

STOLEN THEN RETURNED?

THAT'S RIGHT...AND I HAVEN'T THE FOGGIEST. WE OUGHT TO X-RAY THEM AGAIN TO SEE IF THE EGYPTIANS MISSED SOMETHING OR SOMETHING WAS SLIPPED IN AT THE AIRPORT.

CAIRO

CUSTOMS - CUSTOMS - CUSTOMS - CUSTOMS - CUSTOMS - CUSTO

THERE HAS TO BE A REASON SOMEONE WENT TO SO MUCH TROUBLE!

MAYBE NOT. I EVER TELL YOU ABOUT THE CRIME SPREE I ONCE HAD? THE TIME SOMEONE WAS DESTROYING APPLE JUICE DELIVERY TRUCKS?

WE TRIED TO FIGURE OUT WHY HE WAS DOING IT. TURNED OUT HE JUST HATED APPLE JUICE. THE JUDGE SENTENCED HIM TO FIVE-TO-TEN YEARS OF HARD CIDER.

THAT DID NOT HAPPEN.

OF COURSE NOT! I JUST WANT YOU TO LIGHTEN UP! I'LL ORDER X-RAYS FOR THE MUMMIES! MAYBE WE'LL GET THEIR PROSTATES CHECKED WHILE WE'RE AT IT!

The x-rays reveal nothing...

NO HIDDEN JEWELS, MICROFILM, EXPLOSIVES, BIOLOGICAL WEAPONS... THEY DON'T EVEN HAVE PROSTATES!

THEN MY JOB IS DONE HERE. I'LL SEE YOU LATER, DOLAN! CALL ME WHEN YOU HAVE A MORE INTERESTING ASSIGNMENT!

HOME? BY WAY OF VITO'S PIZZERIA?

NOT JUST YET. I WANT TO FOLLOW SOME MUMMIES TO THEIR FINAL STOP--THE MUSEUM OF NATURAL HISTORY!

THANK YOU FOR ALL YOU DID TO GET THEM HERE, SPIRIT! OUR EGYPTIAN EXHIBIT HAD A SEVERE DEFICIENCY OF MUMMIES!

GLAD TO HELP FILL IT, PROFESSOR!

TO ANSWER YOUR QUESTION: NO, THE TRANSACTION FOR THEM WAS *QUITE ROUTINE!* A BROKER OFFERED US A GOOD PRICE AND WE ACCEPTED!

WELL, I HOPE THEY ENJOY THEIR NEW HOME!

VITO'S? I HAVE TERMINAL JET LAG! I THINK I NEED *SLEEP* MORE THAN I NEED *PIZZA!*

MAN, YOU *MUST BE* TIRED!

Later that evening, as the Spirit sleeps...

CENTRAL CITY METROPOLITAN MUSEUM

SO WHAT'S IT GONNA BE TONIGHT, RUDY? LENO OR LETTERMAN?

I'M IN A CRANKY MOOD. LET'S WATCH LETTERMAN.

RUDY! THAT LADY JUST *FAINTED!* I KNOW WE'RE NOT SUPPOSED TO UNLOCK THE DOOR AFTER 11, BUT SHE'S GOT A *BABY...*

THEY WON'T OBJECT. JUST THIS ONCE!

LADY? ARE YOU ALL RIGHT?

LEMME GET A LOOK AT HER! I THINK WE'RE GONNA NEED AN *AMBULANCE!*

MAKE ONE MOVE AND YOU *WILL* NEED AN AMBULANCE! BUT NOT FOR *ME!*

BOTH OF YOU! GET INSIDE AND YOU WON'T GET HURT! I'M GOING TO TIE YOU UP!

EASY DOES IT!

Within moments...

JUST SIT THERE, WATCH TV AND DON'T TRY TO GET LOOSE!

HERE-- I'LL SWITCH OVER TO LENO! HE HAS A BETTER MONOLOGUE!

And supervising it all from a limousine outside...

PERFECT! EVERYTHING ACCORDING TO PLAN! IT MAKES ME WISH I COULD BE THERE TO SEE THE LOOK ON THE SPIRIT'S FACE WHEN HE FIGURES IT ALL OUT!

...THAT IS, *IF* HE FIGURES IT ALL OUT!

YOU'RE STEALING THE *MUMMIES* WE JUST GOT IN!

HEY, YOU'RE SMART TO FIGURE THAT OUT!

THEY DON'T HIRE JUST *ANYBODY* FOR THESE SECURITY GUARD JOBS!

NO, BUT THEY HIRE GUYS SMART ENOUGH TO DIAL A PHONE...

BEEP BOOP BEEP

LARRY? CALL THE COPS, QUICK! THE MUMMIES HERE AT THE MUSEUM--THEY'RE BEING *STOLEN!*

Within seconds, the police are alerted...

Uh, COMMISSIONER DOLAN? THIS IS BLAINE AT DISPATCH!

I HATE TO WAKE YOU UP AT THIS HOUR AND I'VE ALREADY DISPATCHED OFFICERS TO HANDLE IT... BUT I THOUGHT YOU'D WANT TO KNOW...

WHAT??!!

WHAT'S *THE SPIRIT'S* NUMBER? NEVER MIND. I HAVE IT ON SPEED-DIAL!

RRRRRINGG

GOTTA BE DOLAN SAYING SOMEONE STOLE THE MUMMIES AGAIN.

One fast shower later...

YOU OUTSIDE? GREAT. WE NEED TO GET BACK TO THE MUSEUM *A.S.A.P.* AND NO, WE CAN'T STOP AT VITO'S ON THE WAY!

As soon as possible...

I DON'T WANT *EXCUSES!* I WANT *ANSWERS!*

IF I WERE YOU, I'D TAKE WHAT I CAN GET! RIGHT NOW, IT'S EXCUSES!

THAT CRIME SCENE PHOTOG GIVES ME AN IDEA, SPIRIT...

HAS ANYONE THOUGHT TO COMPARE PHOTOS OF THE MUMMIES *BEFORE* THEY WERE STOLEN IN EGYPT WITH PHOTOS OF THEM *AFTER* THEY WERE RETURNED?

I HAVE! THAT IDEA HIT ME AS I WAS GETTING READY FOR BED, AND I COMPOSED AN E-MAIL TO THE MUSEUM ASKING THEM TO ASSEMBLE PHOTOS LIKE THAT!

I FIGURED OUT HOW TO PHRASE IT AND WHO TO SEND IT TO...

...AND THEN I FELL ASLEEP BEFORE I DID.

DO YOU HAVE THAT PALMBERRY THING OF YOURS? LET'S SEND A MESSAGE AND HAVE THEM UPLOAD PHOTOS TO DOLAN'S OFFICE!

It's three hours before the images arrive...

CAN YOU ZOOM IN ON THAT ONE?

WASTE OF TIME IF YOU ASK ME.

SOMETHING *HAS* TO BE DIFFERENT ABOUT THE MUMMIES! THE GUYS IN EGYPT DIDN'T STEAL THEM TO TAKE THEM OUT TO A MOVIE!

HOLD IT! THAT ONE *RIGHT THERE!*

I DON'T SEE ANY DIFFERENCE.

THE MUMMIES WERE *REWRAPPED.* THE WRAPPING ON THEM AFTER THEY WERE RETURNED TO THE MUSEUM IN EGYPT IS SIMILAR BUT *NOT THE SAME!*

I BELIEVE YOU'RE RIGHT.

I DON'T SEE IT, BUT IT'S 3:30 IN THE MORNING. I'LL TAKE YOUR WORD FOR IT!

YOU MAY HAVE HELPED BLOW THIS CASE WIDE OPEN, EBONY. WHY SO GLUM?

'CAUSE VITO'S CLOSES AT THREE. BACK TO THE MUSEUM, RIGHT?

*R*ight...

SO... WHAT ARE WE LOOKING FOR?

DON'T KNOW. A CLUE OF SOME SORT...

HOW'S THAT SECURITY CAMERA FOR ONE? BUT I GUESS THE MUSEUM ALREADY STUDIED WHATEVER IT PHOTOGRAPHED!

THAT'S NOT THE MUSEUM'S. IT BELONGS TO THAT LIQUOR STORE! *COME ON!*

Fortunately, it's an all-night shop...

I PUT THAT IN AFTER THE ELEVENTH TIME I WAS ROBBED! IT'S HELPED A LITTLE.

NOW I ONLY GET ROBBED EVERY *OTHER* WEEK!

THE CAMERA FEEDS TO A VCR HERE IN THE BACK ROOM...THAT IS, WHEN MY WIFE ISN'T TAPING *AMERICAN IDOL* ON IT!

IT'S EXTRA SLOW SPEED TO GET A LOT ON ONE TAPE, BUT AS YOU CAN SEE, THE IMAGE ISN'T *TOO* BAD...

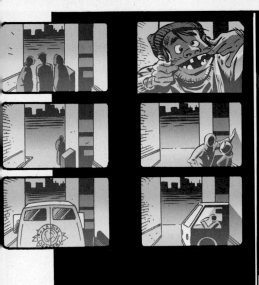

RIGHT THERE! *STOP IT!* EBONY, SEE IF YOU CAN READ THE NAME ON THAT VAN!

06-08-08 01:36

It says "Rosario's Cleaners" and the plant is six blocks away...

THERE'S THE ADDRESS, BOSS! AND THERE'S THE VAN!

IT COULD HAVE JUST BEEN A GUY WHO WORKS HERE WHO STOPPED AT THAT STORE TO BUY SMOKES!

DIDN'T YOU NOTICE? THE TIME STAMP ON THE SURVEILLANCE TAPE MATCHED THE TIME OF THE ROBBERY!

THERE'S ONE OF THE MUMMIES AND I DON'T THINK HE'S HERE TO BE FLUFFED AND FOLDED!

SOMEONE BEHIND ME...

SORRY, BUT I HAVE THIS THING AGAINST BEING SHOT!

SO WHAT HAVE WE HERE--?

PAPER? ALL THIS WAS ABOUT PAPER?

TIME FOR LIGHTS OUT, SPIRIT!

GOOD MORNING, SPIRIT! IF THE BACK OF YOUR HEAD ACHES, IT'S NOT A MIGRAINE. THAT'S WHERE MY MAN HIT YOU!

OCTOPUS! THIS HAS ALL BEEN ONE OF YOUR SLEAZY ENTERPRISES?

I'D PREFER TO CALL IT A *BUSINESS VENTURE*... AND I REALLY MUST COMPLIMENT YOU! YOU *ALMOST* DISRUPTED IT IN RECORD TIME!

BOSS! WE HAVE ALL THE PAPER LOADED IN THE TRUCK! YOU READY TO HAVE ME TAKE CARE OF OUR NEW MUMMY HERE?

BUT IT'S NOT *PAPER*, IS IT, OCTOPUS? YOU STOLE THE MUMMIES AND REWRAPPED THEM IN THE HIGHEST-GRADE EGYPTIAN LINEN...

...THE MATERIAL ON WHICH INTERNATIONAL BONDS OF TRADE ARE PRINTED!

CORRECT! YOU WERE SEARCHING ON THE *INSIDES* OF THE MUMMIES AND OVERLOOKING THE *OUTSIDES*!

TWELVE MUMMIES... I'M GUESSING FORTY FEET OF LINEN PER MUMMY... THAT WORKS OUT TO...

HELP ME. I'M NOT GOOD AT MATH WHEN I HAVE A SPLITTING HEADACHE!

IT'S ENOUGH TO PRINT FORTY, PERHAPS *FIFTY* MILLION DOLLARS' WORTH OF BONDS, DEPENDING ON SPOILAGE!

AND *YOU* WON'T STOP ME! YOU'LL BE ON EXHIBIT AT THE MUSEUM!

"ON EXHIBIT?"

WE'RE GOING TO REWRAP THE MUMMIES AND RETURN THEM... SO THE POLICE WON'T BE LOOKING FOR THEM!

BUT ONE OF THE MUMMIES *BROKE* WHEN WE UNWRAPPED HIM HERE... SO WE NEED A *NEW BODY* INSIDE!

THAT'S WHERE *YOU* COME IN!

DON'T WORRY... YOU WON'T FEEL A THING. NOW OR EVER AGAIN.

OCTOPUS WAS LUCKY TO FIND ME AND I WAS LUCKY TO GET THIS JOB.

YOU'D BE AMAZED HOW LITTLE CALL THERE IS FOR A GUY WHO KNOWS HOW TO DO MUMMIFICATION!

I'M REAL GOOD AT IT! I USED TO PRACTICE ON MY *HOUSE PETS* WHEN THEY DIED...

I WAS *ALL EXCITED* WHEN GRANDMA KICKED OFF, BUT MY FOLKS SAID, "NO WAY!" IN FACT, YOU'RE MY FIRST HUMAN! NOW, *HOLD STILL...*

SORRY! CAN'T DO THAT!

NEXT TIME, CHECK THE POCKETS BEFORE YOU TRY MUMMIFYING SOMEONE!

DON'T *LEAVE*, BOYS!

YOU CAN WATCH ME ARREST YOUR EMPLOYER!

BECAUSE IT'S ABOUT TIME...

...SOMEONE DID!

OCTOPUS IS TRYING TO GET AWAY OUTSIDE! HOPE EBONY'S PAYING ATTENTION!

DRIVE ME FAR FROM HERE! NOW!

RIGHT AWAY, SIR!

THE VAN'S PULLING OUT! I GOT A HUNCH THE SPIRIT--

--WOULD WANT ME TO DO THIS!

Police arrive and quickly nab everyone...

...everyone EXCEPT The Octopus...

I DON'T KNOW *HOW* HE GOT AWAY AGAIN...

...BUT AT LEAST WE BROKE UP THE WHOLE SCHEME! THE EGYPTIAN CONSULATE SAYS THEY'RE SENDING A "THANK YOU" GIFT...

I'M JUST GLAD IT'S OVER. I NEVER WANT TO SEE ANOTHER MUMMY AS LONG AS I LIVE!

MAYBE EVEN LONGER THAN *THAT!*

YOU SEEM HAPPY, EB.

JUST TALKED TO MY TAXI COMPANY! LOOKS LIKE I'M GETTING A BRAND NEW CAB OUT OF ALL THIS!

SO EVERYONE'S HAPPY.

PACKAGE FOR THE SPIRIT. FROM THE EGYPTIAN CONSULATE.

AH, MY REWARD! MAYBE THEY SENT ME SOME RARE WINE OR PRICELESS ARTIFACT!

LET'S OPEN IT AND HAVE A LOOK!

FRAGILE

I'D SAY IT'S YOU!

THIS WILL GO GREAT IN YOUR APARTMENT!

ALL RIGHT!

THE END

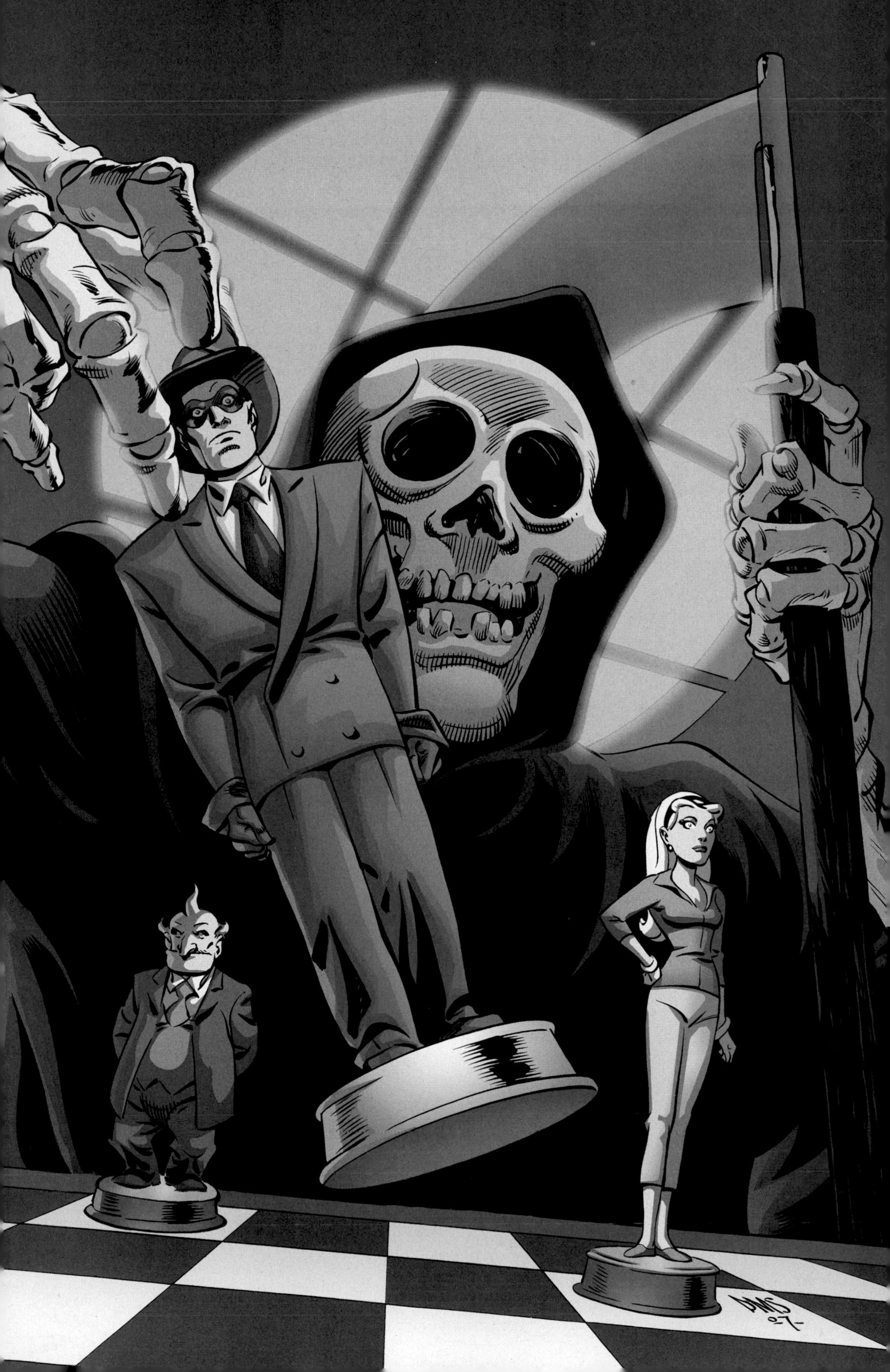

Art by Paul Smith & Lee Loughridge

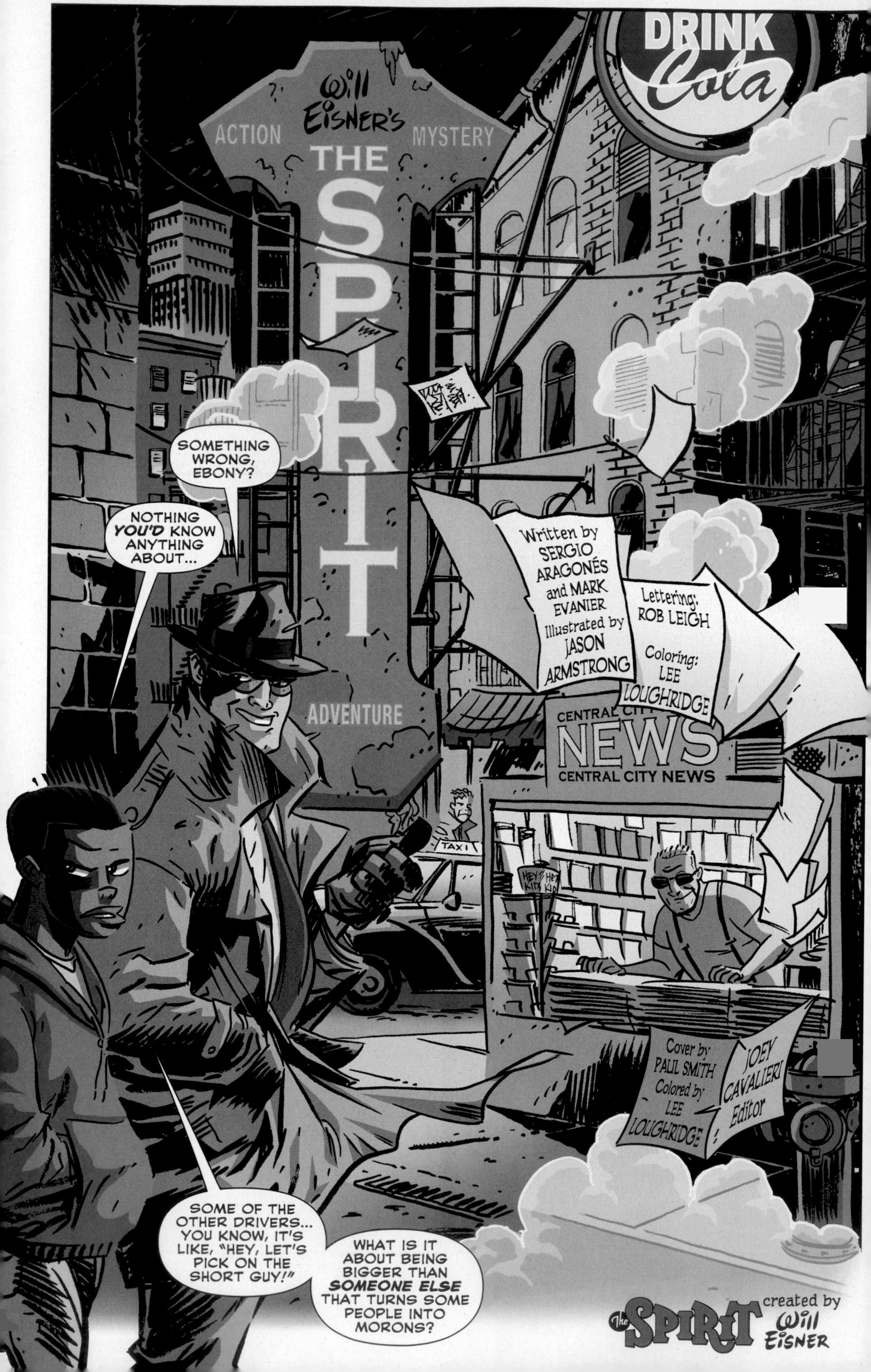
DRINK Cola
Will Eisner's
ACTION
MYSTERY
THE SPIRIT
ADVENTURE
SOMETHING WRONG, EBONY?
NOTHING YOU'D KNOW ANYTHING ABOUT...
Written by SERGIO ARAGONÉS and MARK EVANIER
Illustrated by JASON ARMSTRONG
Lettering: ROB LEIGH
Coloring: LEE LOUGHRIDGE
CENTRAL CITY NEWS
NEWS
CENTRAL CITY NEWS
TAXI
Cover by PAUL SMITH
Colored by LEE LOUGHRIDGE
JOEY CAVALIERI Editor
SOME OF THE OTHER DRIVERS... YOU KNOW, IT'S LIKE, "HEY, LET'S PICK ON THE SHORT GUY!"
WHAT IS IT ABOUT BEING BIGGER THAN SOMEONE ELSE THAT TURNS SOME PEOPLE INTO MORONS?
The SPIRIT created by Will Eisner

CONTRARY TO WHAT YOU SEEM TO THINK, I'VE HAD EXPERIENCE WITH BULLIES.

YOU? NO WAY.

IT HAPPENS TO EVERYONE! NO MATTER HOW BIG YOU ARE, THERE'S SOMEONE WHO'S BIGGER--OR THINKS HE IS!

THE USUAL, SAM!

HERE YOU GO, MY FRIEND... THE EVENING TIMES JUST THE WAY YOU LIKE IT-- FROM THE BOTTOM OF THE PILE!

HEY, THAT BLIND DUDE IS SHARP! HE RECOGNIZED YOUR VOICE!

FUNNY YOU SHOULD BRING UP THAT TOPIC JUST NOW! SAM THERE USED TO BE THE BULLY IN MY LIFE!

A BLIND GUY THREATENED TO BEAT YOU UP? Ooh, YOU MUST'VE BEEN REAL SCARED!

THIS WAS BEFORE HE LOST HIS SIGHT...BACK IN ELEMENTARY SCHOOL, IN FACT! THE TWO OF US GO WAY BACK...

I'M PICTURING YOU IN FIFTH GRADE...A LITTLE KID WITH A MASK AND A BLUE HAT!

DUE TO SKIPPING A FEW GRADES, I WAS THE SMALLEST KID IN MY CLASS...

"...SO OF COURSE, SAM USED TO BULLY ME AROUND, BUT HE WASN'T ALL BAD. ONCE IN A WHILE, HE LET ME KEEP MY LUNCH MONEY..."

HEY, WIMP! I WANT A QUARTER FROM YOU TOMORROW...

...OR ELSE!

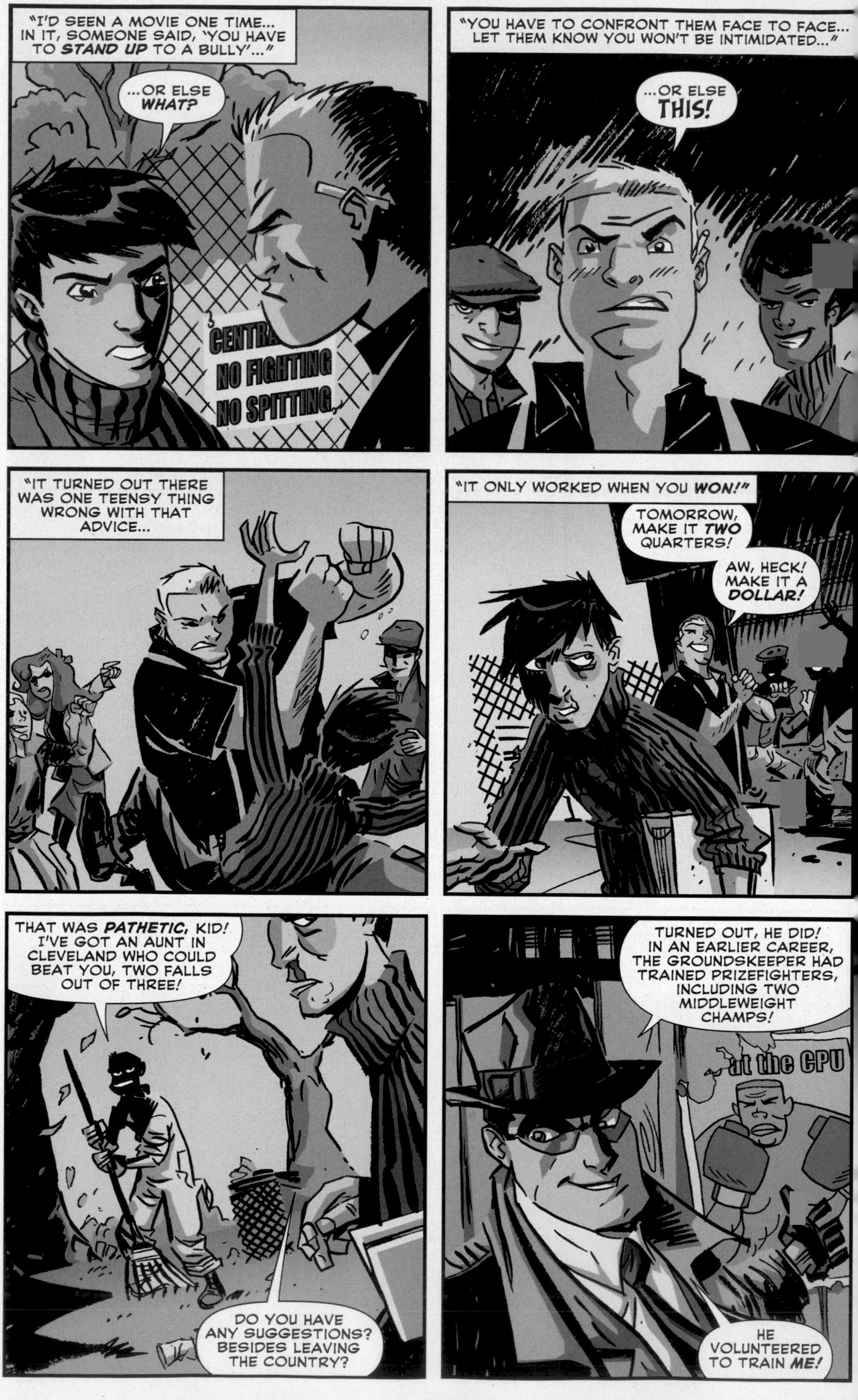
"I'D SEEN A MOVIE ONE TIME... IN IT, SOMEONE SAID, 'YOU HAVE TO *STAND UP* TO A BULLY'..."
...OR ELSE *WHAT?*
CENTRA
NO FIGHTING
NO SPITTING
"YOU HAVE TO CONFRONT THEM FACE TO FACE... LET THEM KNOW YOU WON'T BE INTIMIDATED..."
...OR ELSE **THIS!**
"IT TURNED OUT THERE WAS ONE TEENSY THING WRONG WITH THAT ADVICE...
"IT ONLY WORKED WHEN YOU *WON!*"
TOMORROW, MAKE IT *TWO* QUARTERS!
AW, HECK! MAKE IT A *DOLLAR!*
THAT WAS *PATHETIC,* KID! I'VE GOT AN AUNT IN CLEVELAND WHO COULD BEAT YOU, TWO FALLS OUT OF THREE!
DO YOU HAVE ANY SUGGESTIONS? BESIDES LEAVING THE COUNTRY?
TURNED OUT, HE DID! IN AN EARLIER CAREER, THE GROUNDSKEEPER HAD TRAINED PRIZEFIGHTERS, INCLUDING TWO MIDDLEWEIGHT CHAMPS!
at the CPU
HE VOLUNTEERED TO TRAIN *ME!*

"WHEN HE WASN'T CLEANING UP OUR SCHOOLYARD, HE WORKED AT A GYM DOWN ON LEXINGTON...

FASTER!

HARDER!

STRONGER!

"THEY LET HIM USE IT WHENEVER HE WANTED. SO, EVERY DAY AFTER SCHOOL, WE'D BE DOWN THERE, AND OFTEN ON THE WEEKENDS..."

DON'T TELL ME! THE NEXT TIME SAM TRIED BULLYING YOU, YOU KNOCKED HIS BLOCK OFF!

THAT'S HOW I THOUGHT IT WOULD GO, BUT THINGS TURNED OUT A LITTLE DIFFERENT! THERE WAS A DAY I THOUGHT I WAS READY TO TAKE HIM...

...BUT I COULDN'T DO IT ON THE SCHOOL GROUNDS! I FIGURED I'D WIN AND THEN GET EXPELLED! SO I WENT OVER TO HIS HOUSE...WHERE A FIGHT WAS ALREADY IN PROGRESS...

THAT MUST BE SAM'S OLD MAN...

"IT WAS EASY TO SEE WHERE SAM GOT IT-- LIKE FATHER, LIKE SON..."

I'LL TEACH YOU TO TALK BACK TO ME! YOU WON'T DO *THAT* AGAIN!

"HIS FATHER WAS ONLY DOING TO HIM WHAT HE'D DONE TO ME SO MANY TIMES, AND YET STANDING THERE...WATCHING IT LIKE THAT...

"WELL, I JUST FINALLY HAD TO SAY SOMETHING..."

ONLY A **COWARD** FIGHTS WITH SOMEONE SMALLER THAN HE IS!

"NOT THE BRIGHTEST THING I EVER SAID BUT, HEY, I WAS JUST A KID..."

"FOR A FEW MINUTES THERE, IT DIDN'T LOOK LIKE I'D GET ANY OLDER..."

ANOTHER PUNK! DON'TCHA HAVE NO RESPECT FOR YOUR **ELDERS**?

ONLY THE ONES DESERVING OF RESPECT!

"FORTUNATELY, I WAS READY FOR IT-- PHYSICALLY **AND** EMOTIONALLY..."

YOU'RE GONNA BE SORRY YOU MEDDLED--

NO, **YOU'RE** THE ONE WHO'S GONNA BE SORRY! ON ACCOUNT OF YOU'RE A SORRY EXCUSE FOR A FATHER!

"I THINK HE WAS MORE STUNNED THAN HURT..."

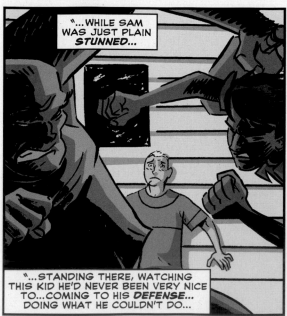

"...WHILE SAM WAS JUST PLAIN **STUNNED**...

"...STANDING THERE, WATCHING THIS KID HE'D NEVER BEEN VERY NICE TO...COMING TO HIS **DEFENSE**... DOING WHAT HE COULDN'T DO..."

"...BUT I HAD **THREE** ADVANTAGES OVER HIM. FIRST, THERE WERE ALL THOSE WEEKS OF TRAINING...

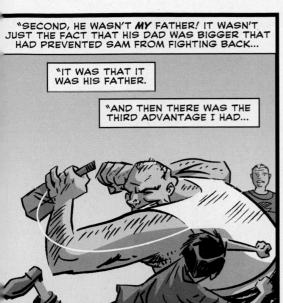

"SECOND, HE WASN'T *MY* FATHER! IT WASN'T JUST THE FACT THAT HIS DAD WAS BIGGER THAT HAD PREVENTED SAM FROM FIGHTING BACK...

"IT WAS THAT IT WAS HIS FATHER.

"AND THEN THERE WAS THE THIRD ADVANTAGE I HAD...

"I HAD A LOT OF PENT-UP ANGER...ANGER AT BIG GUYS PICKING ON LITTLE GUYS...

"AND NOW I HAD A PLACE TO PUT IT."

HAD ENOUGH?

YOU'RE A GOOD FIGHTER, KID...

WISH MY BOY WAS MORE LIKE THAT!

HE IS.

ACTUALLY, HE'S MORE LIKE *YOU!* HE'S BEEN BEATIN' THE TAR OUTTA ME FOR MONTHS NOW! WHICH MEANS HE COULD BEAT *YOU* UP...

...BUT HE DOESN'T.

FOR SOME REASON I SURE CAN'T UNDERSTAND, HE SEEMS TO LOVE YOU.

GET OUTTA HERE WITH THAT KINDA TALK!

SEE YOU IN SCHOOL TOMORROW, SAM! I WON'T BE GIVING YOU ANY QUARTERS!

"THE NEXT DAY AT SCHOOL, I MADE IT CLEAR TO SAM'S FRIENDS THAT I WOULDN'T BE SLAPPED AROUND ANY LONGER..."

"THEY WAITED FOR SAM TO PUT ME IN MY PLACE, BUT..."

SAM! POUND HIM!

SHOW HIM WHO'S BOSS!

"BUT SAM JUST SMILED."

AND FROM THAT DAY FORWARD, WE WERE FRIENDS! SAM WENT ON TO BECOME A PRETTY GOOD PROFESSIONAL BOXER...UP UNTIL THE TIME HIS EYES STARTED TO FAIL... I BUY A PAPER FROM HIM *EVERY DAY* AND SOMETIMES, HE GIVES ME A LEAD ON A CASE! HE *OVERHEARS* THINGS...

SO SINCE HE KNEW YOU BEFORE YOU WERE THE SPIRIT, HE KNOWS WHO THE SPIRIT IS...

HE KNOWS THE VOICE OF HIS FRIEND, AND HE KNOWS I'M INVOLVED IN POLICE WORK...

WHETHER HE KNOWS WHO THE SPIRIT IS, I HAVE NO IDEA! THERE ARE ONLY A FEW PEOPLE WHO KNOW!

ANYWAY, DON'T LET YOUR BULLIES BULLY YOU, EBONY! AND I HOPE YOU'VE LEARNED SOMETHING FROM THIS STORY!

YEAH. IF A GUY'S GIVING YOU TROUBLE, GO OVER TO HIS HOUSE AND BEAT UP HIS PARENTS.

CCPD

THE END

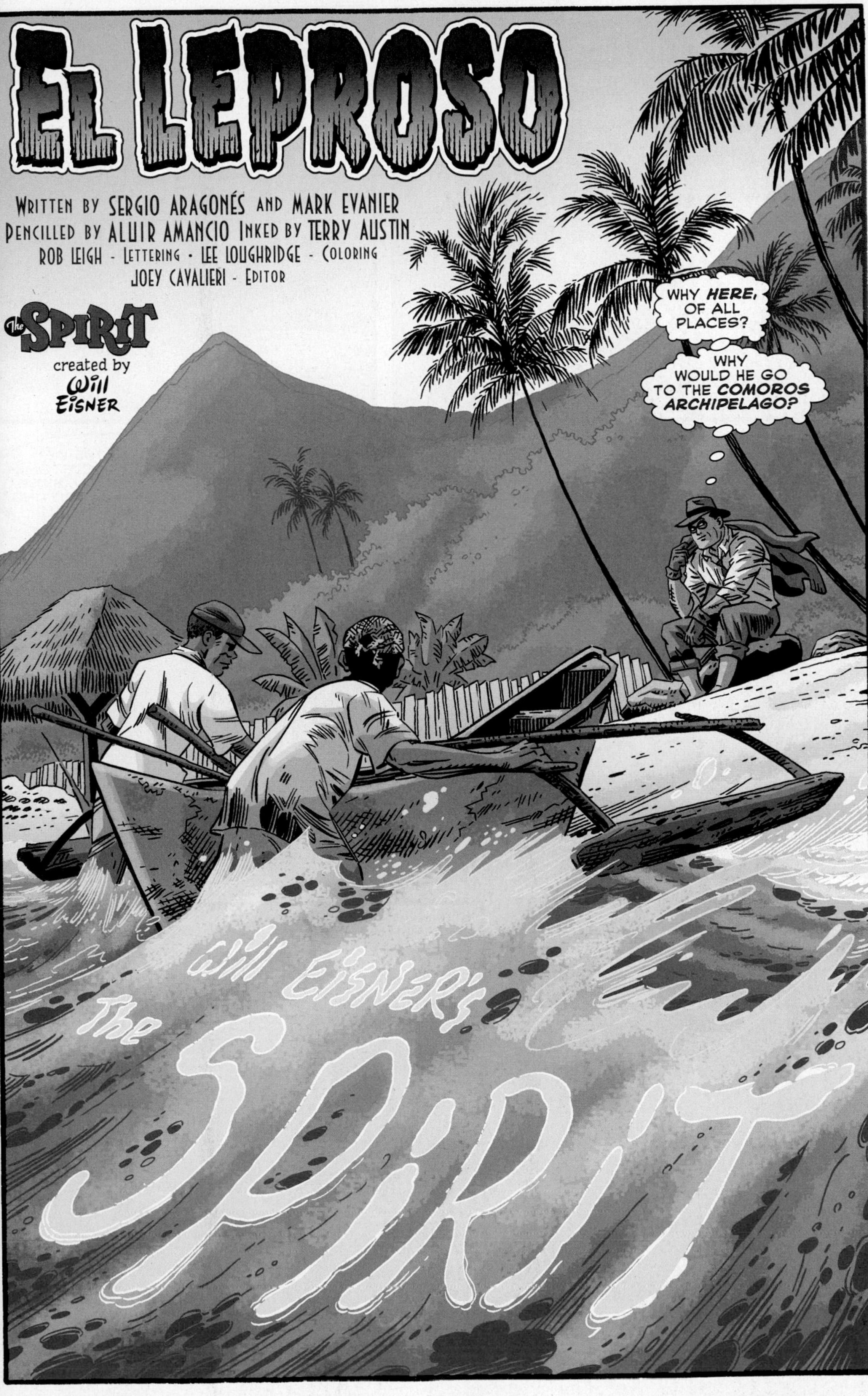
EL LEPROSO
WRITTEN BY SERGIO ARAGONÉS AND MARK EVANIER
PENCILLED BY ALUIR AMANCIO INKED BY TERRY AUSTIN
ROB LEIGH - LETTERING - LEE LOUGHRIDGE - COLORING
JOEY CAVALIERI - EDITOR
The SPIRIT created by Will Eisner
WHY HERE, OF ALL PLACES?
WHY WOULD HE GO TO THE COMOROS ARCHIPELAGO?
Will Eisner's The SPIRIT

FISH, MISTER?

NO, THANKS! I LIKE SUSHI AS MUCH AS THE NEXT GUY, BUT THAT'S A LITTLE TOO FRESH FOR ME!

I KNOW WHY I'M HERE, STARING AT THE INDIAN OCEAN! I'M HERE TRYING TO FIND HIM...

...BUT WHAT IN THE NAME OF ROBINSON CRUSOE COULD HAVE POSSESSED HIM TO COME HERE?

MAYBE HE DIDN'T. DOLAN SAID IT WAS AN "UNCONFIRMED REPORT"...

STILL LOOKING FOR EL LEPROSO? I DON'T KNOW...

A GUY WHO'D DO WHAT HE DID TO AVOID PRISON... THAT'S A PRETTY HARD GUY TO CATCH...

WELL, MAYBE WE GOT LUCKY. A CUSTOMS AGENT IN MOZAMBIQUE SPOTTED A MAN FITTING HIS DESCRIPTION...

THE U.S. DOESN'T HAVE AN EXTRADITION AGREEMENT WITH THE COMOROS!

FIND HIM. DRAG HIM SOMEWHERE YOU CAN ARREST HIM AND DO SO!

NOT EXACTLY KOSHER... BUT THEN NEITHER WAS HIS ROBBING ALL THOSE BANKS...

I CAN'T DECIDE IF WHAT DOLAN WANTS ME TO DO IS ETHICAL, LEGAL, MORAL OR SOME OF THE ABOVE. I'LL DECIDE AFTER I GET MY MAN...

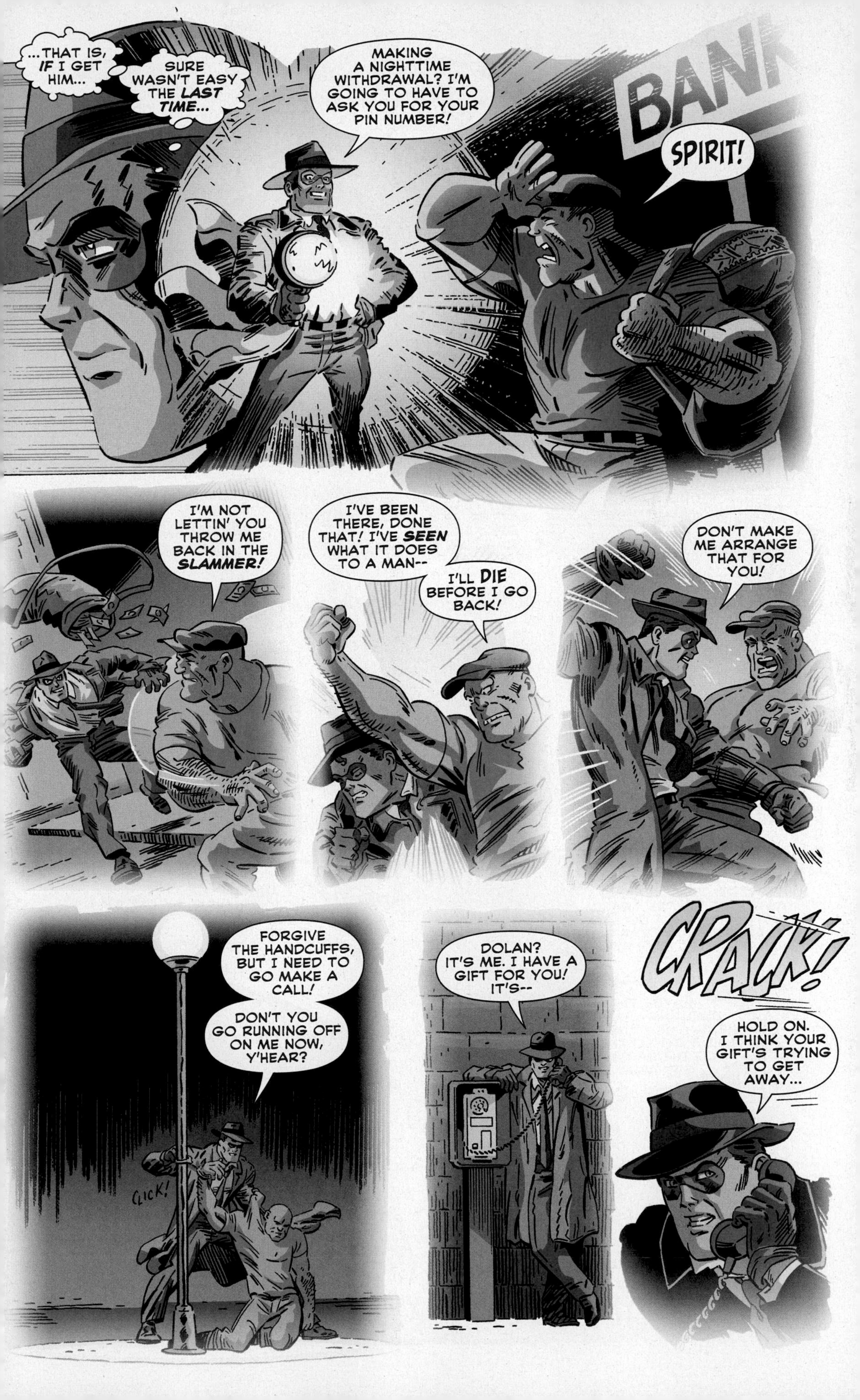
...THAT IS, *IF* I GET HIM...
SURE WASN'T EASY THE *LAST TIME*...
MAKING A NIGHTTIME WITHDRAWAL? I'M GOING TO HAVE TO ASK YOU FOR YOUR PIN NUMBER!
BANK
SPIRIT!
I'M NOT LETTIN' YOU THROW ME BACK IN THE *SLAMMER!*
I'VE BEEN THERE, DONE THAT! I'VE *SEEN* WHAT IT DOES TO A MAN--
I'LL **DIE** BEFORE I GO BACK!
DON'T MAKE ME ARRANGE THAT FOR YOU!
FORGIVE THE HANDCUFFS, BUT I NEED TO GO MAKE A CALL!
DON'T YOU GO RUNNING OFF ON ME NOW, Y'HEAR?
CLICK!
DOLAN? IT'S ME. I HAVE A GIFT FOR YOU! IT'S--
CRACK!
HOLD ON. I THINK YOUR GIFT'S TRYING TO GET AWAY...

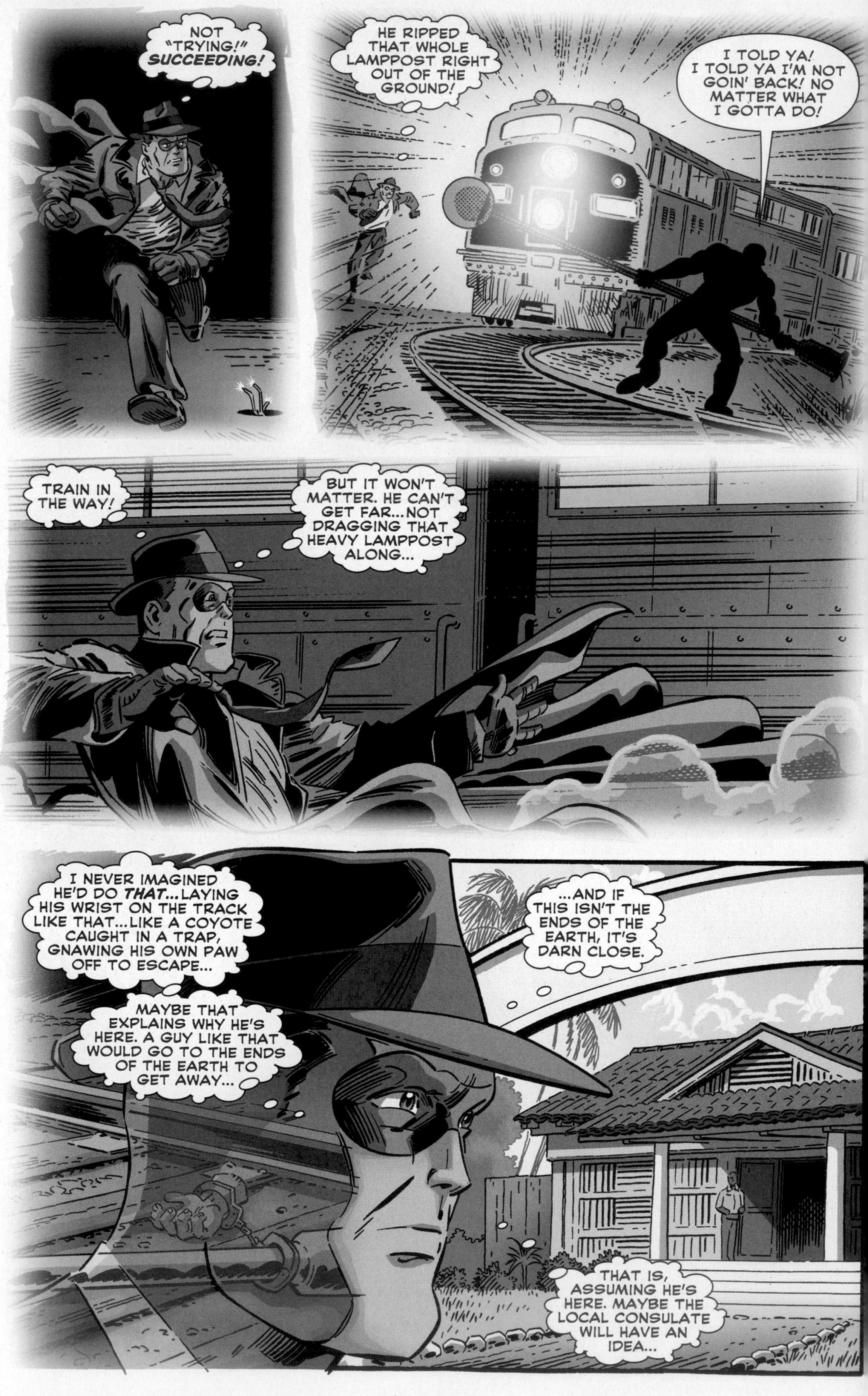
NOT "TRYING!" SUCCEEDING!
HE RIPPED THAT WHOLE LAMPPOST RIGHT OUT OF THE GROUND!
I TOLD YA! I TOLD YA I'M NOT GOIN' BACK! NO MATTER WHAT I GOTTA DO!
TRAIN IN THE WAY!
BUT IT WON'T MATTER. HE CAN'T GET FAR...NOT DRAGGING THAT HEAVY LAMPPOST ALONG...
I NEVER IMAGINED HE'D DO THAT...LAYING HIS WRIST ON THE TRACK LIKE THAT...LIKE A COYOTE CAUGHT IN A TRAP, GNAWING HIS OWN PAW OFF TO ESCAPE...
MAYBE THAT EXPLAINS WHY HE'S HERE. A GUY LIKE THAT WOULD GO TO THE ENDS OF THE EARTH TO GET AWAY...
...AND IF THIS ISN'T THE ENDS OF THE EARTH, IT'S DARN CLOSE.
THAT IS, ASSUMING HE'S HERE. MAYBE THE LOCAL CONSULATE WILL HAVE AN IDEA...

NO, MY FRIEND... NO CRIMINAL TYPES SUCH AS YOU DESCRIBE!

DON'T GO JUST BY THE MISSING HAND. HE COULD BE WEARING A PROSTHETIC DEVICE OF SOME SORT...

AND IS IT ALWAYS SO HOT HERE?

THIS IS *WINTER* TO US! AND NO, I AM CERTAIN.

THERE IS ONE MAN WHO FITS THE DESCRIPTION, NO RIGHT HAND AND ALL. BUT HE IS A MONK... A MAN OF GREAT PEACE IN THE LEPER COLONY ON SHISIWA UNEFU!

MAYBE I'LL CHECK HIM OUT JUST THE SAME!

A MONK IN A LEPER COLONY? THAT SURE DOESN'T SOUND LIKELY.

THEN AGAIN, NEITHER DOES WHAT HE DID THAT NIGHT ON THE TRAIN TRACKS...AND IT'S NOT LIKE I HAVE ANOTHER LEAD...

NO, IT COULD NOT BE. THE MONK WITH ONE HAND, BROTHER PAOLO, HAS LIVED HERE FOR MORE THAN FIVE YEARS...

EL LEPROSO GOT AWAY SIX YEARS AGO.

HE IS PRACTICALLY A *SAINT* TO THE POPULATION! YOU WILL EXCUSE THE PUN, I TRUST, BUT HE REBUILT THE LEPER COLONY HERE ALMOST *SINGLE-HANDEDLY!*

I EXCUSE THE PUN...BUT HE COULD *STILL* BE THIS WANTED CRIMINAL...

I DO NOT SEE HOW. I MEAN, I CAN IMAGINE HOW IT COULD BE THE *INHABITANT* OF THE SAME BODY THAT ROBBED THE BANKS AND DID THE VIOLENCE OF WHICH YOU SPEAK...

...BUT IT COULD NOT BE THE *SAME MAN.*

THE LAW DOES NOT MAKE THAT DISTINCTION.

THERE ARE HIGHER FORCES THAN LAWS, MY GOOD SIR...

YOU ARE IN OUR LAND NOW. AND IN OUR LAND, IT IS NOT WHAT YOU *WERE* THAT MATTERS AS MUCH AS WHAT YOU *ARE.*

THERE IS BROTHER PAOLO. THEY ARE LAYING THE FOUNDATION FOR THE NEW ORPHANAGE...COMPLETELY FUNDED BY DONATIONS HE HAS RAISED!

NO WONDER YOU THINK OF HIM AS A SAINT.

COULD I HAVE A WORD WITH YOU...

...EL LEPROSO?

NO...NOT NOW... IT IS NOT GOING TO HAPPEN...

I'LL **TELL YOU** WHAT'S GOING TO HAPPEN...

YOU'RE GOING TO PUT THIS TOWARDS BUILDING YOUR ORPHANAGE.

'BYE.

THE TIP WAS GOOD, DOLAN. IT **WAS** EL LEPROSO, BUT I GOT THERE TOO LATE! HE DIED SOME TIME AGO.

JUST AS WELL, I GUESS. SAVES US THE EXPENSE OF A TRIAL, TO SAY NOTHING OF LOCKING THE GUY AWAY FOR ALL ETERNITY.

HEY, DOLAN-- JUST OUT OF CURIOSITY...

DO YOU THINK A GUY LIKE THAT COULD **CHANGE?** BECOME SOMEONE DECENT AND RESPECTED AND CARING?

A PIECE OF HUMAN SCUM LIKE EL LEPROSO? **NEVER.**

IT'S NICE TO THINK ABOUT, SPIRIT, BUT IT JUST DOESN'T HAPPEN...

A LEOPARD DOESN'T CHANGE HIS SPOTS.

EL LEPROSO

THE END

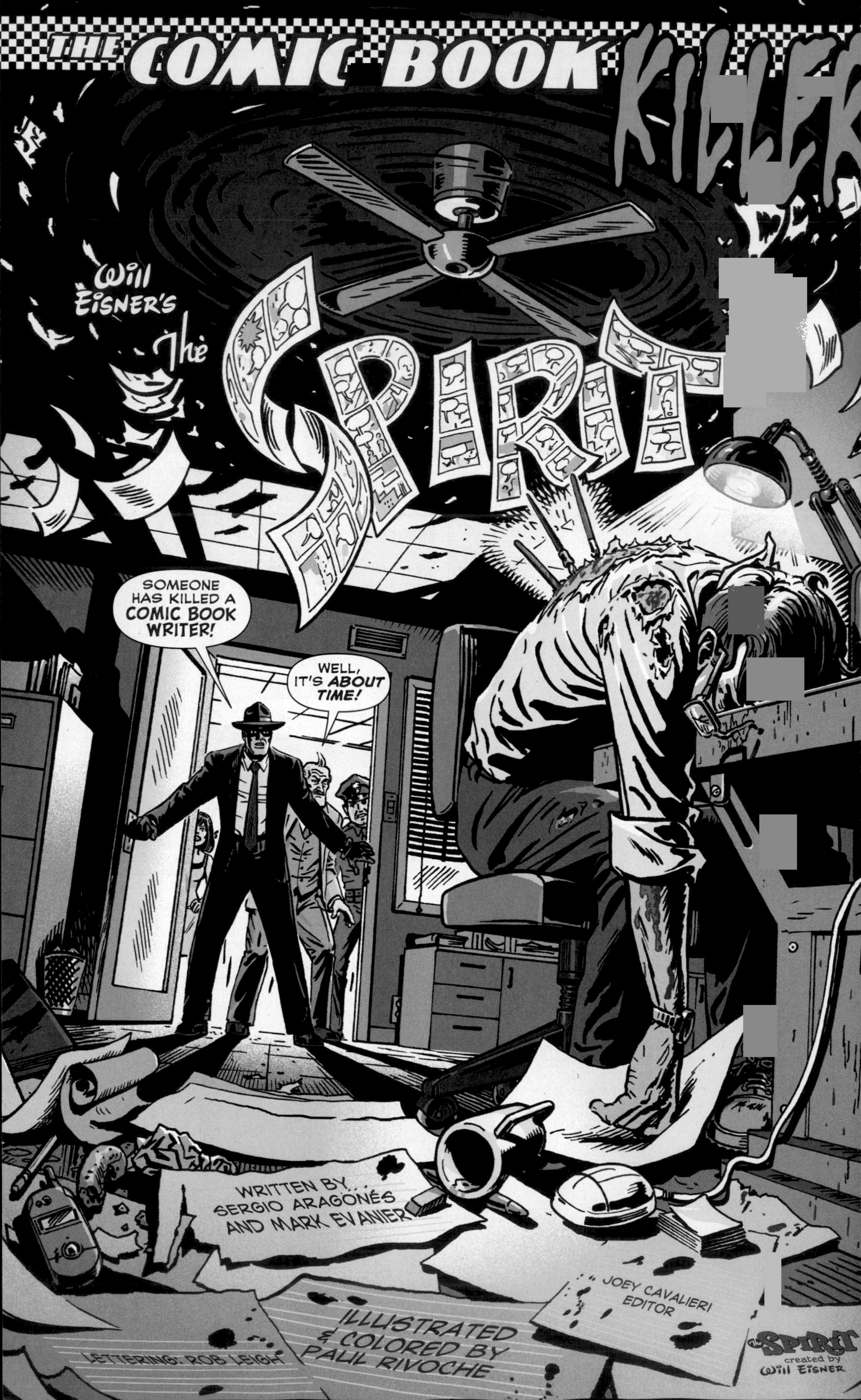
THE COMIC BOOK KILLER
Will Eisner's The SPIRIT
SOMEONE HAS KILLED A COMIC BOOK WRITER!
WELL, IT'S ABOUT TIME!
WRITTEN BY... SERGIO ARAGONÉS AND MARK EVANIER
JOEY CAVALIERI EDITOR
ILLUSTRATED & COLORED BY PAUL RIVOCHE
LETTERING: ROB LEIGH
The SPIRIT created by Will Eisner

I DON'T MEAN IT'S ABOUT TIME SOMEONE KILLED HIM! I MEAN IT'S ABOUT TIME *YOU GOT HERE*, SPIRIT! I SENT FOR YOU AN *HOUR* AGO!

I COULDN'T GET A *CAB!* EBONY WAS MAKING A RUN TO THE AIRPORT.

SO! STABBED THREE TIMES WITH THREE PENS...ANY IDEA WHO DID IT?

ISN'T IT *OBVIOUS* WHO DID IT?

MAYBE TO YOU...

WELL, HE WAS STABBED *THREE TIMES* AND *THREE MEN* HAVE CONFESSED TO THE CRIME! SURELY EVEN THE *CITY'S FINEST* CAN DO THE MATH ON THAT ONE!

YOU'RE THE EDITOR HERE, RIGHT?

RIGHT. I SAW HIM ALIVE TEN MINUTES BEFORE THEY MUST HAVE DONE THE STABBING! ALL THREE WERE ARTISTS WHO WORKED WITH HIM!

WHERE ARE THESE THREE ARTISTS?

DOWN AT THE STATION! THEY'RE ALL DICTATING THEIR CONFESSIONS!

DOESN'T SOUND LIKE YOU NEED ME, THEN...UNLESS YOU SUSPECT ALL IS NOT AS IT APPEARS?

I DON'T KNOW *WHAT* I SUSPECT. THESE COMIC BOOK PEOPLE ARE SO STRANGE! I DON'T THINK *READING THEM* DRIVES YOU TO VIOLENCE...

...BUT *WRITING THEM* SURE COULD.

WELL, THIS ONE *LOOKS* NORMAL!

A LOT OF PEOPLE DO... AND THEN YOU FIND OUT THEY HAVE THEIR GRANDMOTHER STUFFED AND MOUNTED IN THE ATTIC!

LET'S LISTEN IN ON THIS GUY...

FOR THE LAST TIME, I'M TELLING YOU! I KILLED HIM BECAUSE HE *DESERVED IT!*

IF YOU DON'T BELIEVE IT, READ HIS *LOUSY SCRIPTS!* I'VE SEEN *UNABRIDGED DICTIONARIES* WITH FEWER WORDS IN THEM!

WORDS EVERYWHERE, FILLING EVERY PANEL, DESCRIBING EVERY BUTTON ON EVERY JACKET... CROWDING OUT MY PICTURES, LEAVING ME NO ROOM TO DRAW!

WHY COULDN'T HE UNDERSTAND THIS IS A *VISUAL MEDIUM?*

PEOPLE DON'T BUY COMIC BOOKS TO READ A LOT OF WORDS! THAT'S WHAT BLOGS ARE FOR!

I DIDN'T KILL HIM BECAUSE I *WANTED TO!*

I KILLED HIM BECAUSE I *HAD TO!*

FOR THE GOOD OF THE ART FORM!

YOU WANT TO SIGN YOUR STATEMENT?

JUST AS LONG AS IT DOESN'T HAVE A LOT OF WORDS IN IT.

I DON'T KNOW, DOLAN. I DON'T THINK A COMIC BOOK CAN HAVE TOO MANY WORDS IN IT...NOT IF THEY'RE NECESSARY TO CONVEY THE PLOT AND TO EXPAND ON THE GRAPHIC STORYTELLING! A PICTURE, AFTER ALL, CANNOT CONVEY CERTAIN INTERNAL OR ABSTRACT CONCEPTS! THAT'S WHY PANTOMIME COMICS AND CARTOONS ARE SO RARELY SUCCESSFUL! IT DOESN'T SOUND TO ME LIKE A VERY CONVINCING MOTIVE TO KILL SOMEONE!

WORDS, WORDS, WORDS! I'M SO SICK OF WORDS!

ALL THOSE WORDS OF HIS! THAT WAS HARDLY THE WORST OF IT!

ALL RIGHT...TAPE'S ROLLING. ANYTHING YOU WANT TO SAY FOR THE RECORD?

ONLY THAT I KILLED HIM AND I'M PROUD OF IT.

CLIK

HE HAD HIS NAME ON THOSE STORIES AS WRITER--BUT ALL HE DID WAS TYPE UP THE DIALOGUE! THE PLOTS...THE CHARACTERS...THEY ALL CAME FROM ME!

HE NEVER HAD AN IDEA IN HIS LIFE! I HAD TO COME UP WITH EVERYTHING SO I'D HAVE SOMETHING TO DRAW...SOME WAY TO EARN A LIVING...

AND THEN, OF COURSE, HE GOT ALL THE CREDIT! HE TOOK BOWS FOR MY WORK! PEOPLE WANTED TO HIRE HIM TO WRITE MOVIES BECAUSE THEY THOUGHT HE HAD SUCH BRILLIANT IDEAS!

WELL, WHAT ABOUT ME? HE WAS GETTING RICH AND I WAS SLAVING AWAY AT THE DRAWING TABLE, DAY AND NIGHT, WATCHING MY EYES GET WORSE AND WORSE...

CAN YOU BLAME ME FOR KILLING HIM?

WELL, YES...

...THAT IS, IF HE DID IT! THE MOTIVES IN THIS CASE SOUND A LITTLE...WHAT'S THE TERM I'M THINKING OF, DOLAN?

"...LIKE A COMIC BOOK!"

AND IF YOU THINK THAT GUY SOUNDED LIKE HE WAS MISSING PARTS, HERE'S THE THIRD ARTIST!

IF YOU'D READ THE COMIC WE DO, YOU'D **KNOW** WHY I WANTED HIM DEAD!

HE TOOK A COMIC CREATED BY A GREAT TALENT AND **DESTROYED IT!**

IT WAS A **CLASSIC!** BUT THEN THE CREATOR DIED AND THIS **HACK** GOT HIS FILTHY HANDS ON IT!

HE CHANGED EVERYTHING TO PUT **HIS** IMPRINT ON IT...TO MAKE IT **HIS!**

HE BUTCHERED THE CHARACTERS! DESTROYED THE ENTIRE CONCEPT! I KNOW THE COMPANY HAS TO MAKE MONEY OFF THEIR WORK, BUT DID THEY HAVE TO GIVE IT TO **HIM?**

KILLING IS **TOO GOOD** FOR SOMEONE LIKE THAT, BUT I ONLY DID TO HIM WHAT HE DID TO A GREAT CHARACTER!

CALM DOWN! WE'LL HAVE YOU SIGN A STATEMENT!

I MAY BE WRONG, BUT I DON'T THINK BEING STABBED WITH INK IS **LETHAL!**

AND WHEN DID THEY DO IT? WHEN HE WAS NAPPING?

IF SOMEONE STABBED ME WITH A PEN, I'D WAKE UP! SOMETHING IS NOT RIGHT HERE.

DO YOU THINK THE THREE OF THEM WERE IN CAHOOTS? THEY ALL STABBED HIM AT THE SAME TIME?

NO...THE ONLY SCENARIO THAT MAKES SENSE TO ME IS THAT WHEN THEY STABBED HIM, HE WAS ALREADY DEAD.

WELL, THE AUTOPSY RESULTS WERE DUE AT THREE AND IT'S 2:58. LET'S GO FIND OUT.

Shortly...

WE FOUND STRONG AMOUNTS IN HIS BLOODSTREAM OF A MIXTURE CONTAINING BOTULINUM...ENOUGH TO KILL HIM IN ABOUT AN HOUR.

THAT WAS IN THE INK?

NO, THAT WAS IN HIS LATTE. HE HAD A WHITE MOCHA LATTE THAT SOMEONE POISONED. IT'S QUITE DEADLY UNLESS ONE GETS THE ANTIDOTE, WHICH IS CALLED TRIVALENT BOTULINUM ANTITOXIN...

WHERE DOES ONE FIND BOTULINUM?

LOOK IN THE FACE OF ANY SUPERMODEL OVER THIRTY. IT'S A COMPONENT OF *BOTOX!* I CAN'T BELIEVE PEOPLE ACTUALLY *PAY* TO BE INJECTED WITH A LETHAL POISON.

MAYBE WE OUGHT TO START QUESTIONING FAMILY MEMBERS... LOOKING FOR SOMEONE WITH A MOTIVE TO KILL HIM...

MAYBE.

I'M HEADING OVER TO HIS HOME. WANNA TAG ALONG?

NO, EBONY'S WAITING FOR ME. I'M GOING TO GO RESEARCH IT FROM ANOTHER ANGLE!

YOU KNOW ME. I GET A HUNCH AND I'VE GOTTA FOLLOW IT UP.

I GOT THE ADDRESS YOU ASKED FOR!

FINE. LET'S GO PAY THE GUY A VISIT AND HOPE HE'S NOT HOME!

And so...

BOY, I THOUGHT COMIC BOOK EDITORS LIVED BETTER THAN THIS.

BOTULINUM! AND I DON'T THINK HE'S PLANNING ON INJECTING ANY SUPERMODELS...

I FOUND ENOUGH TO KNOW I'M RIGHT, BUT NOT ENOUGH TO CONVICT!

TAKE ME TO THE COMIC BOOK COMPANY OFFICE AGAIN! HE'S PROBABLY THERE.

Soon...

YOU'RE CRAZY, SPIRIT! I'M EDITOR-IN-CHIEF HERE AND HIS COMIC WAS VERY SUCCESSFUL FOR US! WHY WOULD I WANT HIM DEAD?

I WAS HOPING YOU'D TELL ME.

SEE THIS LITTLE VIAL? I FOUND IT IN YOUR APARTMENT AND I ADDED SOME TO THE COFFEE YOU'VE BEEN DRINKING!

YOU WHAT!?

QUICK! GET ME TO A HOSPITAL! THERE'S TIME IF I GET THE ANTIDOTE RIGHT AWAY!

IT TAKES ABOUT AN HOUR FOR THAT POISON TO BE EFFECTIVE! HURRY!

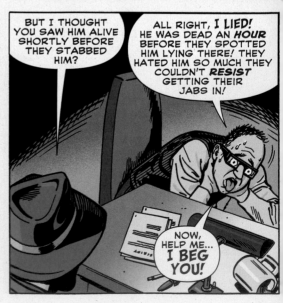

BUT I THOUGHT YOU SAW HIM ALIVE SHORTLY BEFORE THEY STABBED HIM?

ALL RIGHT, I LIED! HE WAS DEAD AN HOUR BEFORE THEY SPOTTED HIM LYING THERE! THEY HATED HIM SO MUCH THEY COULDN'T RESIST GETTING THEIR JABS IN!

NOW, HELP ME... I BEG YOU!

JUST TELL ME **WHY** YOU DID IT!

HIS SCRIPTS **STUNK!** I REWROTE **EVERY WORD** OF THEM BUT HE WAS GETTING ALL THE BENEFITS! **ALL THE BIG OFFERS!**

THE BOOK WAS A HIT AND THE PUBLISHER WOULDN'T LET ME FIRE HIM AND-- **PLEASE!** GET ME THE **ANTIDOTE!**

YOU DON'T NEED IT. I DIDN'T PUT ANYTHING IN YOUR COFFEE! THE ONLY POISON IN YOU IS YOUR OWN GUILT!

COMMISSIONER! DID YOU HEAR WHAT THIS MAN TOLD ME?

LOUD AND CLEAR, SPIRIT. AND I THINK THE TAPE RECORDER GOT IT DOWN, TOO. LET'S READ HIM HIS RIGHTS.

DID I MENTION HE WAS ALWAYS LATE WITH HIS ROTTEN WORK, TOO? EVERYONE IS ALWAYS LATE!

HOLD IT! BEFORE YOU TAKE HIM AWAY, I HAVE ONE MORE IMPORTANT QUESTION!

I KNOW YOU'RE GOING AWAY FOR A LONG TIME, BUT WHO WOULD I TALK TO HERE ABOUT GETTING ON YOUR COMPANY'S COMP LIST? GETTING THE COMICS FOR FREE?

SPIRIT!

HEY, COMMISSIONER! HAVE YOU SEEN THE PRICE OF COMIC BOOKS LATELY? TALK ABOUT CRIMINAL ACTIVITY!

THE END

Art by Paul Smith & Lee Loughridge

DING DONG

YOU IN THERE, BOSS? READY TO GO?

...where the neighbors are very, very quiet...

...and where a cab driver has come to pick up his favorite fare...

SO... WHERE ARE WE GOING AND WHO'S DEAD?

THE AQUARIUM AND NO ONE'S DEAD... I HOPE.

ELLEN CALLED AND ASKED ME TO JOIN HER THERE! SAID IT WAS URGENT!

WHAT COULD BE URGENT AT AN AQUARIUM? AN ATTACK BY A BUNCHA MAD SUSHI CHEFS?

WE'LL FIND OUT WHEN WE GET THERE.

I ALWAYS THOUGHT AQUARIUMS WERE KINDA CREEPY! EVERY ONE I WAS EVER IN HAD A SNACK BAR THAT SOLD FISH SANDWICHES!

THAT'S WEIRD.

ISN'T IT? IT'S LIKE, "IF YOU DON'T PERFORM WELL, YOU WIND UP ON A BUN, COVERED WITH TARTAR SAUCE!"

LIFE'S LIKE THAT AT TIMES.

THE CENTRAL CITY AQUARIUM AND MARINE HABITAT: On the weekends, a bustling mass of families and tourists...

I DIDN'T COME HERE ON A DATE!

On weekdays, the scene of endless field trips from local elementary schools...

This is a weekday...

SURE YOU DON'T WANT TO COME IN WITH ME?

I'M SURE. I DON'T LIKE FISH, PLUS YOU AND ELLEN WANT TO BE ALONE!

AT LEAST, I DON'T *THINK* I DID!

SO WHERE'S EVERYONE RUNNING IN A HURRY?

ELLEN SAID SHE HAD A DIRE SITUATION AND I WAS THE *ONLY ONE* IN THE WORLD WHO COULD HELP HER WITH IT!

ODDS ARE *ANYONE* COULD HAVE HELPED HER WITH IT, BUT SHE WANTS ME AROUND...

SPIRIT! I KNEW YOU'D COME!

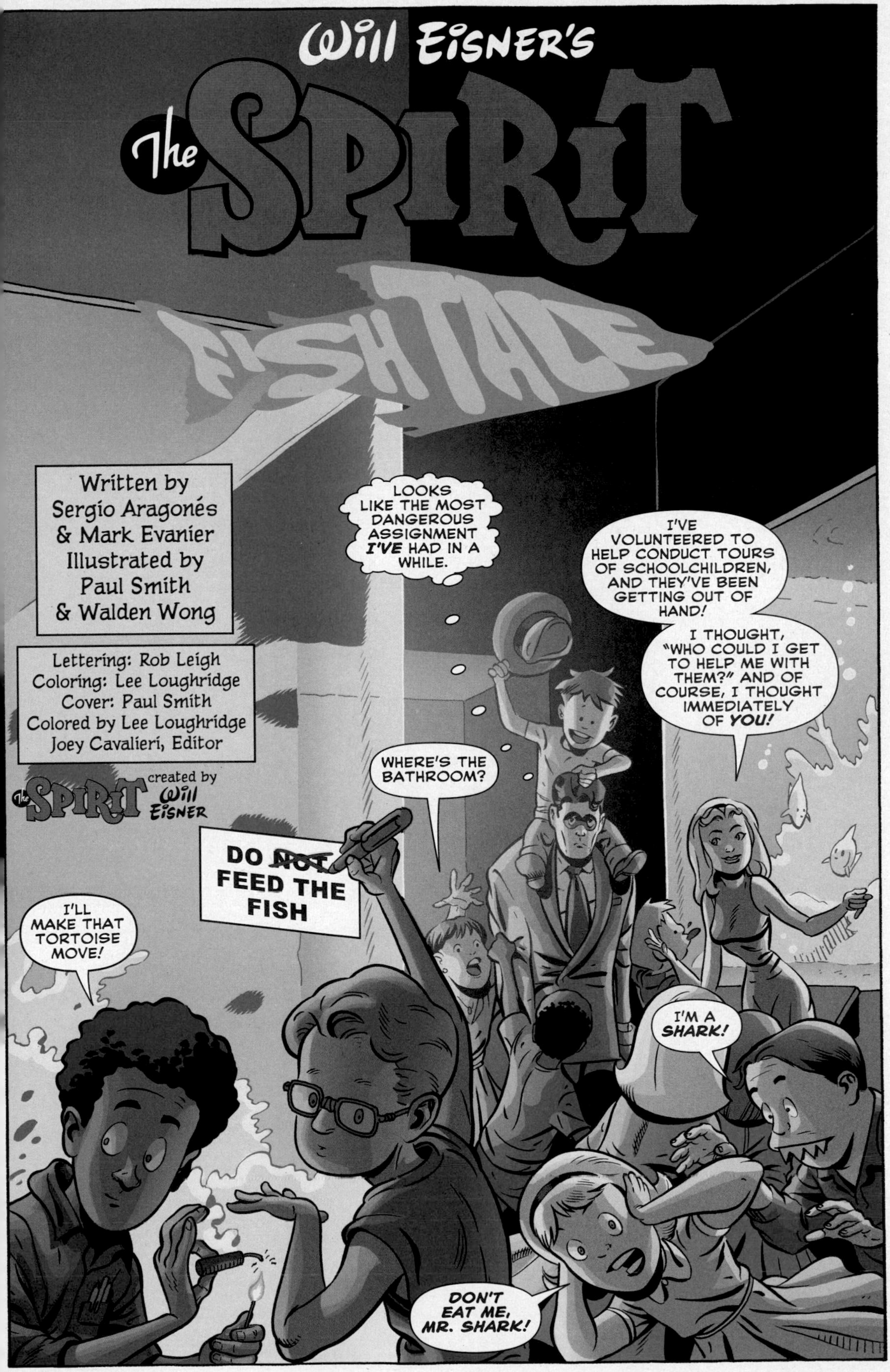
Will Eisner's
The SPIRIT
FISH TALE
Written by Sergio Aragonés & Mark Evanier Illustrated by Paul Smith & Walden Wong
Lettering: Rob Leigh Coloring: Lee Loughridge Cover: Paul Smith Colored by Lee Loughridge Joey Cavalieri, Editor
The Spirit created by Will Eisner
LOOKS LIKE THE MOST DANGEROUS ASSIGNMENT I'VE HAD IN A WHILE.
I'VE VOLUNTEERED TO HELP CONDUCT TOURS OF SCHOOLCHILDREN, AND THEY'VE BEEN GETTING OUT OF HAND!
I THOUGHT, "WHO COULD I GET TO HELP ME WITH THEM?" AND OF COURSE, I THOUGHT IMMEDIATELY OF YOU!
WHERE'S THE BATHROOM?
DO NOT FEED THE FISH
I'LL MAKE THAT TORTOISE MOVE!
I'M A SHARK!
DON'T EAT ME, MR. SHARK!

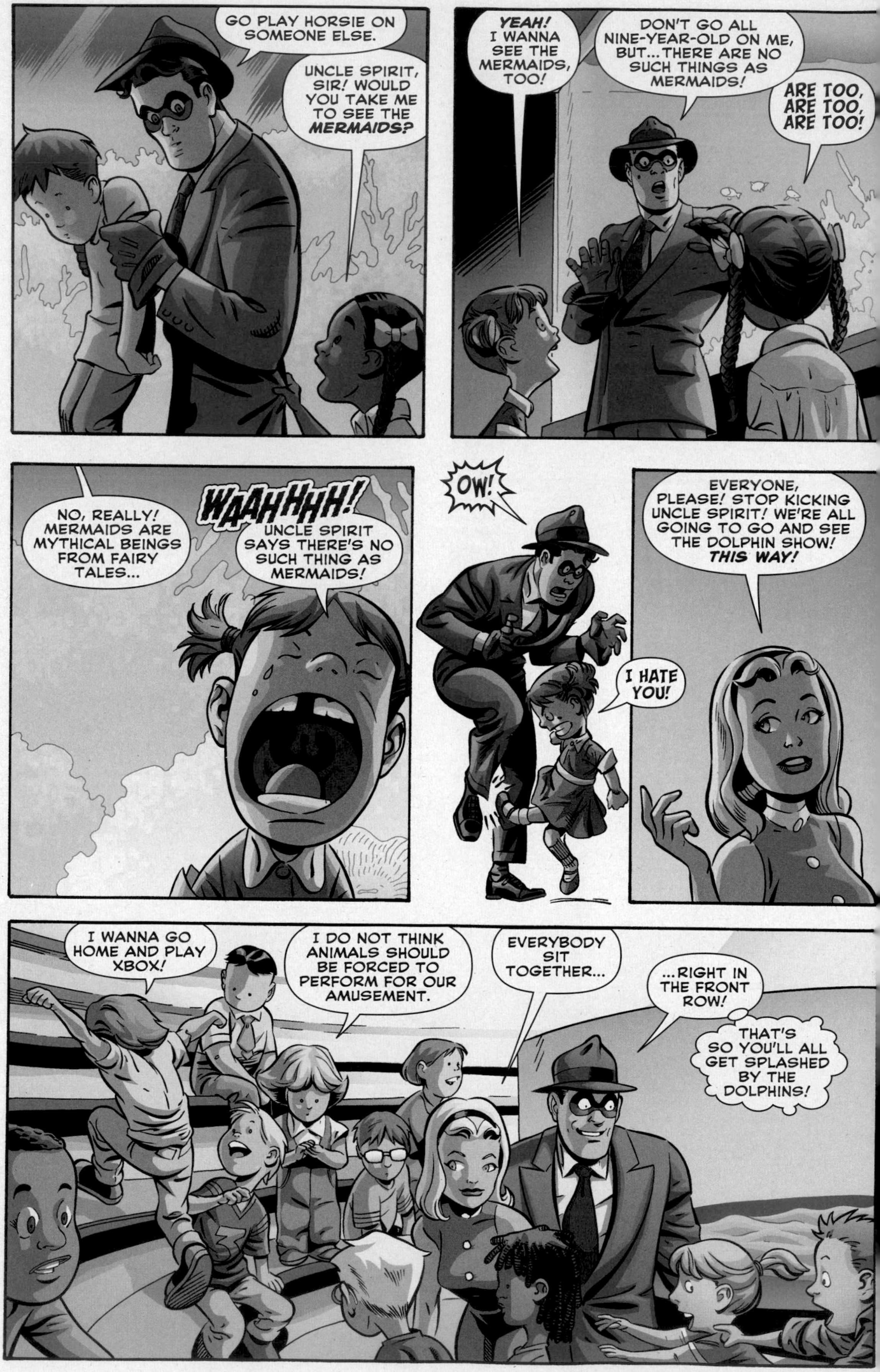
GO PLAY HORSIE ON SOMEONE ELSE.
UNCLE SPIRIT, SIR! WOULD YOU TAKE ME TO SEE THE *MERMAIDS?*
YEAH! I WANNA SEE THE MERMAIDS, TOO!
DON'T GO ALL NINE-YEAR-OLD ON ME, BUT...THERE ARE NO SUCH THINGS AS MERMAIDS!
ARE TOO, ARE TOO, ARE TOO!
NO, REALLY! MERMAIDS ARE MYTHICAL BEINGS FROM FAIRY TALES...
WAAHHHH!
UNCLE SPIRIT SAYS THERE'S NO SUCH THING AS MERMAIDS!
OW!
I HATE YOU!
EVERYONE, PLEASE! STOP KICKING UNCLE SPIRIT! WE'RE ALL GOING TO GO AND SEE THE DOLPHIN SHOW! *THIS WAY!*
I WANNA GO HOME AND PLAY XBOX!
I DO NOT THINK ANIMALS SHOULD BE FORCED TO PERFORM FOR OUR AMUSEMENT.
EVERYBODY SIT TOGETHER...
...RIGHT IN THE FRONT ROW!
THAT'S SO YOU'LL ALL GET SPLASHED BY THE DOLPHINS!

HEY! WHERE ARE THE DOLPHINS?

WHAT'S THAT LADY SAYING?

...SORRY YOU WON'T BE ABLE TO SEE OUR DOLPHIN SHOW TODAY...

WHAT?

MAYBE THEY GAVE THE DOLPHINS THE DAY OFF!

...BUT WE HERE AT THE CENTRAL CITY AQUARIUM AND MARINE HABITAT DO HOPE YOU'LL ENJOY OUR OTHER FINE ATTRACTIONS AND STORES...

...AND IF YOU SHOULD HAPPEN TO SEE ANY POLICE OFFICERS ON THE PREMISES, DON'T PAY ANY ATTENTION TO THEM. THANK YOU.

CANCELLING THE DOLPHIN SHOW? "POLICE"? SOMETHING'S WRONG. SOMETHING'S VERY WRONG.

LET'S TAKE THE KIDS OVER TO WATCH THE OCTOPUS FEEDING!

I THINK I SHOULD GO FIND OUT WHAT THE PROBLEM IS...ESPECIALLY THE PART ABOUT POLICE OFFICERS ON THE PREMISES...

ALL RIGHT, EVERYONE! IT'S OCTOPUS TIME!

I GOTTA GO POTTY!

ALL RIGHT, EVERYONE! WE'RE GOING POTTY AND THEN IT'S OCTOPUS TIME!

COME BACK, UNCLE SPIRIT! COME BACK!

WE LOVE YOU.

ANIMAL TRAINERS DON'T CANCEL PERFORMANCES UNLESS THERE'S A REAL GOOD REASON! THE ANIMALS FORGET THEIR ROUTINES...

EXCUSE ME, SIR. CAN YOU TELL ME WHAT'S--

HEY, *OUTTA HERE*, PAL! NO ONE ADMITTED EXCEPT THE POLICE!

BUT I *AM* THE POLICE... SORT OF.

OW!

"OW"...THAT'S CLEVER! YOU THINK OF IT ALL BY YOURSELF?

SHOW ME WHERE THE TROUBLE IS!

THIS WAY!

ARE YOU THE AUTHORITIES? I CAN HELP YOU!

PLEASE DO.

BUT FIRST, TELL ME WHO YOU ARE.

VICTORIA BAKER... AND I GUESS I'M NOW THE HEAD DOLPHIN TRAINER HERE. SO SAD WHAT HAPPENED TO APRIL...

WHO'S APRIL?

APRIL WAS THE TRAINER! I FED 'EM, SHE TRAINED 'EM! HER NAME WAS APRIL TARLETON AND SOMEBODY KILLED HER! JUST MINUTES AGO!

WHERE'S THE BODY?

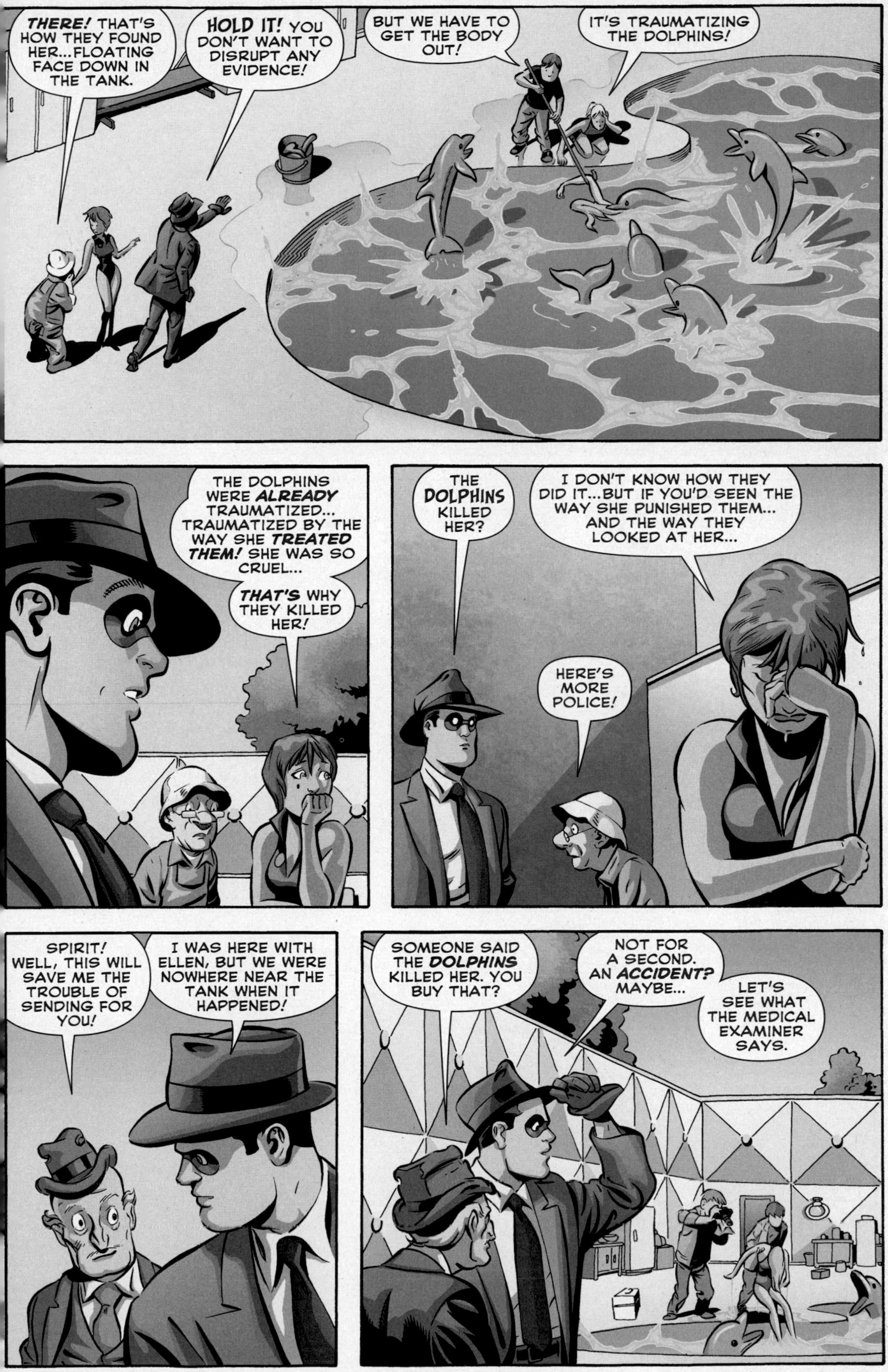
THERE! THAT'S HOW THEY FOUND HER...FLOATING FACE DOWN IN THE TANK.
HOLD IT! YOU DON'T WANT TO DISRUPT ANY EVIDENCE!
BUT WE HAVE TO GET THE BODY OUT!
IT'S TRAUMATIZING THE DOLPHINS!
THE DOLPHINS WERE ALREADY TRAUMATIZED... TRAUMATIZED BY THE WAY SHE TREATED THEM! SHE WAS SO CRUEL...
THAT'S WHY THEY KILLED HER!
THE DOLPHINS KILLED HER?
I DON'T KNOW HOW THEY DID IT...BUT IF YOU'D SEEN THE WAY SHE PUNISHED THEM... AND THE WAY THEY LOOKED AT HER...
HERE'S MORE POLICE!
SPIRIT! WELL, THIS WILL SAVE ME THE TROUBLE OF SENDING FOR YOU!
I WAS HERE WITH ELLEN, BUT WE WERE NOWHERE NEAR THE TANK WHEN IT HAPPENED!
SOMEONE SAID THE DOLPHINS KILLED HER. YOU BUY THAT?
NOT FOR A SECOND. AN ACCIDENT? MAYBE...
LET'S SEE WHAT THE MEDICAL EXAMINER SAYS.

THE DOLPHINS ARE BEHAVING STRANGELY. BUT THERE'S BEEN SOMETHING ODD ABOUT THEM FOR WEEKS NOW.

SIR... WE NEED TO TALK.

FORENSICS

CAUSE OF DEATH: MULTIPLE BLOWS TO THE TEMPOROPARIETAL REGION WITH A BLUNT INSTRUMENT.

IN OTHER WORDS, SOMEONE WHACKED HER ON THE HEAD.

YOU GOT IT.

I'LL KNOW MORE AFTER EXTENSIVE EXAMINATION BUT YOU'VE GOT THE GIST OF IT...

SOMEONE WHACKED HER ON THE HEAD.

WHO WOULD DO SUCH A THING? AND TO SUCH A FINE, SWEET YOUNG WOMAN.

I'VE WORKED HERE FORTY YEARS...NEVER KNEW A BETTER TRAINER...

SO I TAKE IT YOU DON'T THINK THE DOLPHINS WERE RESPONSIBLE. WOULD YOU COME DOWN TO THE STATION, MISTER...UH--?

BLAINE... WALTER BLAINE. AND SURE...IF IT'LL HELP CATCH WHOEVER DID THIS, I'LL COME DOWN, RIGHT AFTER THE 1 PM FEEDING...

I JUST *KNOW* THE DOLPHINS DIDN'T DO ANYTHING...

Half an hour later...

HARD TO TELL WHO'S GRILLING WHO IN THERE! WHO'S ED TALKING TO?

APRIL TARLETON'S BOYFRIEND... WE JUST PICKED HIM UP. NEIGHBORS SAY THEY FOUGHT CONSTANTLY! HE THOUGHT SHE CARED MORE ABOUT THE FISH THAN ABOUT HIM.

I HAVE NEWS.

TEN TO FIFTEEN BLOWS FROM A **BLUNT OBJECT** SHAPED VERY MUCH LIKE THE SNOUT OF A DOLPHIN...AND IT WAS ONE OBJECT OR ONE DOLPHIN! SHE WASN'T STRUCK BY A BUNCH OF DIFFERENT ONES! I CAN GIVE YOU THE EXACT SIZE.

COULD IT HAVE BEEN AN **ACTUAL** DOLPHIN SLAMMING INTO HER? DOLPHINS ARE PRETTY STRONG AND THEIR SNOUTS CAN BE LETHAL! SO I CAN'T SAY IT **COULDN'T** HAVE HAPPENED!

I CAN. IT COULDN'T HAVE HAPPENED.

I'M HEADING BACK TO THE AQUARIUM TO LOOK AROUND SOME MORE.

WELL, **I'M** NOT RULING ANYONE OUT. I WISH, AFTER ED GETS THROUGH WITH THE BOYFRIEND, I COULD HAVE HIM INTERROGATE FLIPPER!

SO WHAT DO YOU THINK, BOSS? DID THE DOLPHINS MEAN TO KILL HER? DID THEY DO IT ON PORPOISE?

EBONY... I WANT YOU TO DO SOMETHING FOR ME. I WANT YOU TO GET A JOB.

A WHAT!!!?

YOU MEAN WORK FOR SOMEONE ELSE? I DRIVE A CAB SO I WON'T HAVE TO DO THAT.

IT'S JUST FOR A BIT...

A JOB AT THE AQUARIUM... I NEED SOMEONE INSIDE TO SNOOP AROUND, FIND OUT THINGS...

YOU ALWAYS SAID YOU'D DO **ANYTHING** FOR ME.

YEAH, BUT THAT WAS WHEN I ONLY EXPECTED TO RUN INTO BURNING BUILDINGS OR DODGE BULLETS! YOU NEVER SAID ANYTHING ABOUT GETTING A J-O-B!

I KNEW I COULD COUNT ON YOU.

And so...

YOU WORK IN HERE, RIGHT? THINK THEY GOT AN OPENING FOR A BROTHER?

IF YOU'RE WILLING TO START AT THE BOTTOM AND PROBABLY GO DOWN FROM THERE.

I HATE IT ALREADY.

COME ON... I'LL INTRODUCE YOU TO THE LADY WHO HIRES THE CREW.

THERE'S AN OLD MAN NAMED BLAINE. HE WAS SUPPOSED TO COME DOWN TO THE POLICE STATION...

OH, DIDN'T YOU HEAR? IT WAS JUST AWFUL! THEY TOOK HIM TO THE HOSPITAL...

EITHER HE SLIPPED OR SOMEONE PUSHED HIM--RIGHT INTO ONE OF THE EMPTY TANKS! THEY SAID HE HAD MULTIPLE FRACTURES AND HEAD INJURIES...

I GOT MY JOB! I START THIS EVENING ON THE NIGHT SHIFT!

GREAT! NOW, BACK TO YOUR DAY JOB! GET ME TO THE HOSPITAL-- FAST!

IF I LET THE GLOBAL POSITIONING SYSTEM PLOT THE FASTEST ROUTE, IT'LL TAKE AN HOUR! IF I JUST DRIVE, TEN MINUTES!

HOW ABOUT IF YOU JUST DRIVE?

Ten minutes later...

NO CHANCE I CAN TALK TO HIM? NOT EVEN FOR A MINUTE?

WE JUST GAVE HIM MORPHINE. THE DOCTOR SAYS HE'LL PULL THROUGH BUT IT'S GOING TO BE ROUGH...

A FEW MINUTES AGO, HE WAS DELIRIOUS...HE SAID SOMETHING ABOUT "APRIL...HOW MUCH THE DOLPHINS LOVED HER..."

I'LL LET YOU KNOW IF HE'S LUCID AGAIN, BUT IT COULD BE WEEKS... IF EVER.

Soon...

WHAT WE CAN DO, COMMISSIONER, IS *TRANQUILIZE* EACH DOLPHIN, ONE AT A TIME. THEN WE CAN MEASURE EACH SNOUT AGAINST THE MEASUREMENTS YOU BROUGHT.

BUT IT'S NOT SOMETHING TO ACCOMPLISH *OVERNIGHT*...

THIS IS THE BIGGEST WASTE OF TIME SINCE I HAD PARIS HILTON IN MY CAB AND TRIED TO DISCUSS QUANTUM PHYSICS!

WE HAVE TO DO IT GENTLY, OF COURSE, SO AS NOT TO HARM THEM...

THAT FELLOW FEEDING THE FISH! ISN'T HE...?

Shhh.

IT WILL BE SAD TO DESTROY THE DOLPHIN THAT KILLED APRIL...

...BUT I AM AFRAID IT MUST BE DONE. AND I AM CERTAIN ONE OF THEM DID IT!

I'M NOT...

NOW, WE MUST RESUME THE DOLPHIN SHOWS... BEFORE THEY FORGET THEIR ACT...

FINE. I'LL JUST TALK TO THE SPIRIT HERE...

SPIRIT?

I HATE IT WHEN HE DOES THAT.

FUNNY... THE DOLPHINS THEY HAVE IN THEIR TANKS HERE ARE ALL BOTTLENECKS. AND YET...

...AMONG ALL THESE FIBERGLASS EXAMPLES OF MARINE LIFE...THEY DON'T HAVE A SINGLE BOTTLENECK...

...UNLESS THERE WAS ONE *THERE*.

EBONY...KEEP AN EYE OUT FOR A FULL-SIZED FIBERGLASS DOLPHIN, MUCH LIKE THE ONES IN THE TANK.

AND TELL *ME!* ARE YOU ENJOYING YOUR JOB HERE?

THIS JOB? HATE IT. I'M TOO USED TO BEING MY OWN BOSS...

ON THE OTHER HAND, ALL THESE FISH, LIVE AND DEAD...THEY STILL SMELL BETTER THAN SOME OF THE FARES I'VE HAD IN MY CAB.

HANG IN THERE. I'M GOING TO CATCH A LITTLE SHUTEYE!

Shortly...

ONLY WAY IT MAKES SENSE... SOMEONE USED A DOLPHIN SCULPTURE TO BEAT THE LADY TO DEATH...

MAYBE WE'LL GET LUCKY. EBONY'LL FIND IT AND IT'LL BE COVERED WITH FINGERPRINTS...

WOULDN'T *THAT* MAKE THINGS EASY?

...WHICH IS EXACTLY WHY IT *WON'T* HAPPEN...

RRING RRING

EBONY? WHAT IS IT?

I'LL BE THERE AS FAST AS I CAN.

HE SAYS HE DIDN'T FIND THE DOLPHIN BUT IT'S URGENT.

WONDER WHAT HE *DID* FIND.

One cab ride later...

YOU WANNA EXPLAIN WHY I HAD TO COME PICK YOU UP IN A CEMETERY?

NO.

KEEP THE CHANGE.

MUCH PRETTIER THAN EBONY... *AND A BETTER* DRIVER...

BOSS! *IN HERE!*

I NOTICED SOMEONE HAD TIED UP THE NIGHT WATCHMAN...FIGURED IT PROBABLY WASN'T THE DOLPHINS...

GOOD DEDUCTION.

Uh, HELLO? HELP?

THEY BACKED THESE TWO LARGE TRUCKS UP TO THE LOADING DOCK A HALF HOUR AGO...

THEY'RE PUTTING TWO OF THE DOLPHINS INTO THAT TRUCK.

Uh-huh. THEY ALREADY HAVE TWO IN THE OTHER TRUCK! WANNA BUST 'EM NOW?

NO...I WANT TO SEE WHERE THEY'RE TAKING THEM. YOU'RE BACK TO BEING A CAB DRIVER!

THANK GOODNESS!

UH, BEFORE YOU GO, GUYS...

LOOKS LIKE THE CRESCENT MARINA...A LOT OF PEOPLE KEEP SMALL BOATS THERE...

HURRY! WE HAVE TO GET THEM BACK TO THE AQUARIUM BEFORE MORNING, AND THERE IS MUCH TO DO!

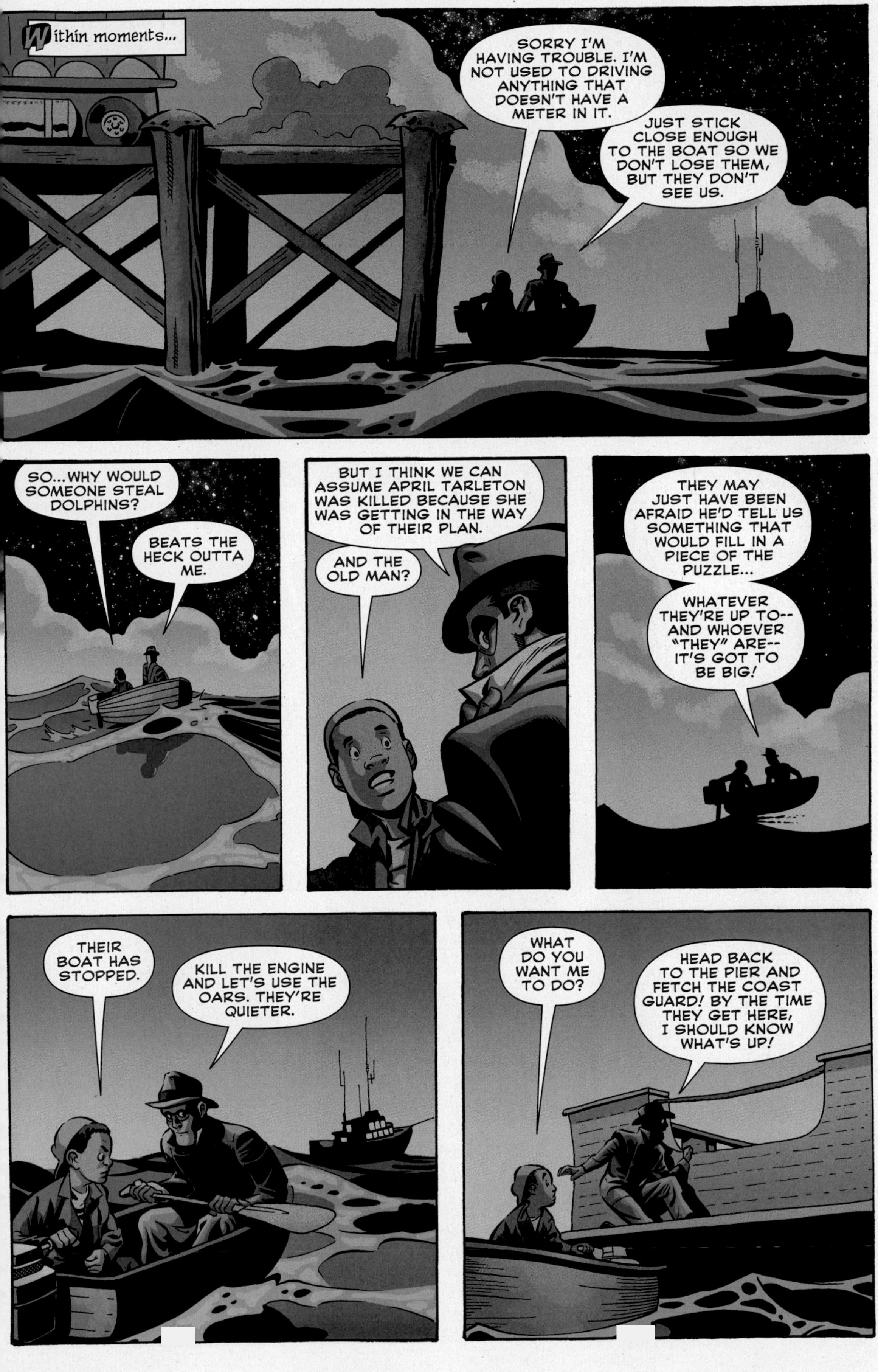
Within moments...
SORRY I'M HAVING TROUBLE. I'M NOT USED TO DRIVING ANYTHING THAT DOESN'T HAVE A METER IN IT.
JUST STICK CLOSE ENOUGH TO THE BOAT SO WE DON'T LOSE THEM, BUT THEY DON'T SEE US.
SO...WHY WOULD SOMEONE STEAL DOLPHINS?
BEATS THE HECK OUTTA ME.
BUT I THINK WE CAN ASSUME APRIL TARLETON WAS KILLED BECAUSE SHE WAS GETTING IN THE WAY OF THEIR PLAN.
AND THE OLD MAN?
THEY MAY JUST HAVE BEEN AFRAID HE'D TELL US SOMETHING THAT WOULD FILL IN A PIECE OF THE PUZZLE...
WHATEVER THEY'RE UP TO-- AND WHOEVER "THEY" ARE-- IT'S GOT TO BE BIG!
THEIR BOAT HAS STOPPED.
KILL THE ENGINE AND LET'S USE THE OARS. THEY'RE QUIETER.
WHAT DO YOU WANT ME TO DO?
HEAD BACK TO THE PIER AND FETCH THE COAST GUARD! BY THE TIME THEY GET HERE, I SHOULD KNOW WHAT'S UP!

I HAVE A HUNCH WHO I'M GOING TO FIND ON BOARD...

DO YOU THINK THEY HAVE HAD ENOUGH TRAINING TO DO IT?

AS I EXPECTED!

BUT OF COURSE...

I "REHEARSED" THEM IN THE TANK AT NIGHT... HAVING THEM BRING UP BOXES OF THE PROPER SIZE...

"BOXES"?

THE HARNESSES ARE SECURE. THEY KNOW WHAT TO DO.

WHAT'S TO STOP THEM FROM JUST SWIMMING AWAY AND NOT COMING BACK TO US?

THEIR TRAINING...

APRIL TAUGHT THEM WELL, BUT I TAUGHT THEM BETTER...AND FOR A MORE "LUCRATIVE" PURPOSE...

CLICK

OH, I HATE THAT SOUND.

WE HAVE AN EXTRA PASSENGER ABOARD.

LET ME OFF ANYWHERE. I'LL WALK HOME.

THE SPIRIT! WHY AM I NOT SURPRISED?

HE MUSTN'T INTERFERE.

MY BABIES ARE READY TO PERFORM ON THE SIGNAL FROM THIS WHISTLE...

TWEET

THEY'LL BRING UP ALL THE BOXES THEY FIND! THEN, WE CAN DECIDE WHAT TO DO WITH OUR VISITOR...

SO IT'S A BIG SALVAGE OPERATION...AND I SUPPOSE APRIL HAD TO BE ELIMINATED BECAUSE SHE FOUND OUT ABOUT IT OR SOMETHING LIKE THAT...

SOMETHING LIKE THAT...

IT LOOKS LIKE YOU DID A GOOD JOB TRAINING THEM, VICTORIA...

YOU THINK SO, JAKOV?

THAT PLEASES ME AS MUCH AS THE SUCCESS OF OUR MISSION!

I THINK I SEE ONE BRINGING UP THE FIRST BOX!

SOON AS I UNHOOK THIS, SEND HIM DOWN AGAIN!

"ОПАСНОСТЬ!" THAT'S ONE OF THEM!

THAT SOUNDED LIKE THE RUSSIAN WORD FOR "DANGER"! WHAT'S IN THOSE BOXES? DRUGS?

WE WOULD NOT GO TO ALL THIS TROUBLE TO SALVAGE DRUGS...

THERE ARE MANY PLACES TO OBTAIN DRUGS...

...BUT ONLY ONE THAT WE KNOW OF TO OBTAIN THE COMPONENTS FOR RADIOLOGICAL DISPERSAL DEVICES...

"DIRTY BOMBS!"

ELEVEN BOXES! I BELIEVE WE HAVE ALL OF THEM NOW...

SO... HOW DO WE GET THE DOLPHINS BACK TO THE AQUARIUM?

WE DON'T. IT WILL BE EASIER TO JUST SHOOT THEM!

WHA--?

THAT'S NOT GOING TO HAPPEN!

BUT IT MUST! THERE IS TOO MUCH AT STAKE!

I'D BETTER MAKE SURE!

OKAY, WHAT DO I DO NOW?

AIR. AIR WOULD BE A GOOD THING...

HE IS ALMOST DEAD, BUT JUST TO BE *CERTAIN*...

MY MOUTHPIECE!

IT'S...LIKE THEY'RE ATTACKING HER...

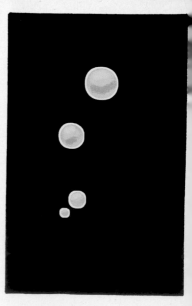

THERE HE IS!

Minutes later...

THAT BOAT...THEY HAVE THE MAKINGS OF DIRTY BOMBS... LIKE *TERRORISTS* USE...

EVERYTHING AND EVERYONE IS IN COAST GUARD CUSTODY. ALL EXCEPT THAT LADY DOLPHIN TRAINER!

I SPOKE TO WARREN AT THE F.B.I. HE SAID THEY'VE BEEN TRACKING THOSE MERCENARIES FOR MONTHS NOW!

HAVE YOUR MEN SEARCH THE MUSEUM! I BET THEY FIND A FIBERGLASS DOLPHIN THAT WAS USED TO CLUB APRIL TARLETON TO DEATH.

I LOOKED AND I DIDN'T SEE IT. BUT I'LL TELL YOU WHAT I *DID* FIND...

THERE WERE BOXES...SAME SIZE AND SHAPE AS THE ONES THEY BROUGHT UP FROM THE OCEAN FLOOR! THEY MUST'VE USED THEM TO TRAIN THE DOLPHINS.

DO YOU THINK THE DOLPHINS KILLED THAT LADY...LIKE FOR REVENGE?

I DON'T KNOW...

...BUT PART OF ME WOULD LIKE TO THINK SO.

Eventually...

THE FIBERGLASS DOLPHIN THEY FOUND IS A PERFECT MATCH FOR THE BLUNT TRAUMAS THAT KILLED APRIL TARLETON.

AND MR. BLAINE IS NOW WELL ENOUGH TO GIVE US A STATEMENT. SO I GUESS WE CAN MARK THIS ONE *"CLOSED!"*

AFTERNOON!

YOU FOUND IT-- IN MY *FORMER* PLACE OF EMPLOYMENT!

SPIRIT! YOU HAVE A WHOLE CROWD THAT'S BEEN WAITING FOR YOU!

REPORTERS? MY ADORING PUBLIC WANTING TO THANK ME FOR BREAKING UP A TERRORIST PLOT?

OH, IT'S BETTER THAN *THAT*...

UNCLE SPIRIT!

CAN YOU TAKE US TO THE *ZOO?*

FIRST, HE'S TAKING EVERYONE FOR ICE CREAM!

TELL US A STORY!

CAN I HAVE YOUR HAT?

THE END

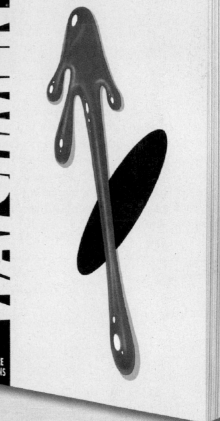